Christian Semiotics and the Language of Faith

Christian Semiotics and the Language of Faith

Alex Scott

iUniverse, Inc.
New York Lincoln Shanghai

Christian Semiotics and the Language of Faith

Copyright © 2007 by Nathan A. Scott III

All rights reserved. No part of this book may be used or reproduced by any means, graphic, electronic, or mechanical, including photocopying, recording, taping or by any information storage retrieval system without the written permission of the publisher except in the case of brief quotations embodied in critical articles and reviews.

iUniverse books may be ordered through booksellers or by contacting:

iUniverse
2021 Pine Lake Road, Suite 100
Lincoln, NE 68512
www.iuniverse.com
1-800-Authors (1-800-288-4677)

The views expressed in this work are solely those of the author and do not necessarily reflect the views of the publisher, and the publisher hereby disclaims any responsibility for them.

ISBN: 978-0-595-42409-2 (pbk)
ISBN: 978-0-595-86745-5 (ebk)

Printed in the United States of America

To Alec and Douglas

Contents

ACKNOWLEDGEMENTS.................................... xi
PREFACE... xiii
Chapter I THE SIGN AS SACRED........................... 1
    The Living Word................................... 2
    Jesus as Symbol of God............................. 3
    Christianity as a Mode of Language................. 3
    The Word as the Light of the World................. 5
    Christian Symbolism................................ 6
    The Theology of Signs.............................. 10
Chapter II THE SIGNIFIER AND THE SIGNIFIED............ 13
    The Theory of the Linguistic Sign.................. 14
    Saussure... 14
    Peirce... 15
    Morris... 16
    Langer... 18
    Whitehead.. 19
    Hjelmslev.. 20
    Eco.. 20
    Sebeok... 22
    The Theory of Codes................................ 22
    Nonverbal Communication............................ 24
    Symbol and Metaphor................................ 25
    Verbal Icons and Iconicity......................... 28
    The Meaning of Signs............................... 29
Chapter III THEMATIC PARADIGMS........................ 31

viii   Christian Semiotics and the Language of Faith

    The Sacramental Sign 32
    The Dynamics of Presence and Absence 35
    The Conflict between Religious Iconism and Iconoclasm 36
    The Visible and the Invisible 37
    The Seen and the Unseen 38
    Body and Spirit 38
    Sin and Righteousness 39
    Faith and Doubt 39
    Signs and Non-Signs 40
    The Power of Sacred Signs. 41
    The Parables of Jesus 42
    The Word of God as Message and Revelation 43
    The Truth of Signs 46
    Anthropomorphism and Gender Symbolism 46
    Other Sacred Signs. 48
    The Semiotics of Interpersonal Dialogue 49

Chapter IV DISCOURSE ANALYSIS 51
    The Sign as a Linguistic Unit or Element. 52
    Text Semiotics. 53
    Foucault's Archaeology 55
    Bakhtin's Theory of Discourse. 57
    Genette's Narrative Theory 58
    The Generative Trajectory of Discourse. 59
    Chomsky's Generative Grammar. 60
    The Tasks of Discourse Analysis 61
    Todorov's Theory of Symbolism 63
    Tagmemics 64
    Biblical Rhetoric and Poetry 64
    Liturgical Language and Speech-act Theory. 66

Chapter V CHRISTIAN SEMIOTICS IN ART AND
   LITERATURE. 70
    Architecture. 71
    Painting. 72

Sculpture..72

Poetry...72

Fiction..73

Drama...73

Music..73

Film...73

Christian Aesthetics...74

Correggio's Ecce Homo..75

Milton's Paradise Lost...77

The Symbolization of Evil..86

The Controversy Concerning Literal vs. Symbolic Interpretation of Scripture..86

Myths and their Symbolic Function...............................87

Dante's Divine Comedy...89

The Christian Imagination..97

Chapter VI CHRISTIAN ETHICS..........................99

The Scope of its Concerns.......................................100

Metaethical Theories..101

Normative Ethical Theories.....................................102

Virtue Ethics...105

Limitations of Normative Theories..............................109

Ethical Codes..110

The Ethical Teachings of Jesus..................................111

Chapter VII ETHICS AND LANGUAGE....................113

The Semiotic Dimensions of Ethical Judgments...............114

The Deontic Modality of Ethical Judgments....................114

Deontic Logic..118

Categories of Deontic Modality.................................119

Christian Love as an Ethical Language.........................123

Chapter VIII CONCLUSION.............................124

Fields of Study for Theological Semiotics.....................125

Limitations and Strengths of Theological Semiotics 128

BIBLIOGRAPHY 131

ACKNOWLEDGEMENTS

I am indebted to the Division of Christian Education of the National Council of the Churches in Christ in the United States of America for permission to use quotations from the Revised Standard Version of the Bible, copyright 1952 (all rights reserved).

I am also indebted to the National Gallery of Art, London for permission to reproduce "Christ Presented to the People (Ecce Homo)" by Antonio Allegri da Correggio.

The discussions of Saussure, Peirce, Morris, Langer, Eco, Buber, Aristotle, and Mill in this book include material from my previously published book, *The Conditions of Knowledge: Reviews of Great Works of Philosophy* (New York: iUniverse, 2006).

PREFACE

What is Christian semiotics? It is a semiotics of Christianity, a study of symbols of faith. It is not an ideology, but an attempt to clarify meaning and signification. It is a theological semiotics, but it is more than a semiotics of theology.

The principal founders of semiotics (the study of signs and symbols) were the Swiss linguist Ferdinand de Saussure (1857-1913) and the American philosopher Charles Sanders Peirce (1839-1914). Other important figures in the development of semiotics included Charles W. Morris (1901-1979), Louis Hjelmslev (1879-1965), Roman Jakobson (1896-1982), Roland Barthes (1915-1980), Umberto Eco (b. 1932), Algirdas Julien Greimas (1917-1992), Julia Kristeva (b. 1941), and Thomas Sebeok (1920-2001). Semiotics has gradually moved from structuralism (in linguistics, anthropology, psychoanalysis, and sociology) to poststructuralism and to text semiotics, making use of communication theory and information theory, and applying itself to many different subjects within the field of cultural studies (including popular culture studies, media theory, sociology, literary theory, and cultural anthropology).

Semiotics as a whole includes many different disciplines, including 1) cultural semiotics, 2) text semiotics, 3) computer semiotics, 4) the semiotics of mathematics and formalized languages, 5) the semiotics of multimedia communication, 6) biosemiotics (the semiotics of biological systems), 7) semiotic sociology, 8) proxemics (the study of the uses that individuals make of interpersonal space in communication), 9) kinesics (the semiotics of gestures, postures, and bodily movements in communication), 10) zoosemiotics (the semiotics of animal communication) 11) the semiotics of visual languages (such as painting and photography), 12) the semiotics of musical codes, 13) medical semiotics, and 14) the semiotics of psychoanalysis and psychiatry.

According to Winfried Nöth (1990), theological semiotics is a branch of text semiotics. Text semiotics includes hermeneutics and exegesis, the study of rhetoric and stylistics, and the semiotics of literature, theater, drama, narrative, myth, theology, and ideology. Text semiotics also includes discourse analysis, text theory, and text linguistics.

Thus, Christian semiotics may be situated within the field of text semiotics. Insofar as it is concerned with the semiotics of Christianity as reflecting (or as reflected by) the whole of society, Christian semiotics may also be placed within the field of cultural semiotics. It may also be placed within the field of philosophical theology.

Christian semiotics is both philosophical and scientific in its aims. It is a linguistic interpretation of Christianity, but not a self-elected or self-proclaimed Christian interpretation of linguistics. It is a study of Christianity as a mode of religious discourse, which examines the linguistic structure and function of Christian religious, moral, social, and aesthetic expression. It is concerned with both symbolic and presentational (or non-symbolic) aspects of Christian faith.

What can we gain from a study of theological semiotics? Semiotics can enable us to gain a deeper understanding of the symbolic function of many aspects of religious faith and worship. Semiotics can also help us to define our beliefs about God by examining our mode of discourse about God. Semiotics can be a useful means of describing the properties and functions of sacred signs and symbols, and it can be a method of exploring the meaning of religious art and ritual. Behavioral semiotics can also help us to understand how religious faith can be translated into moral or social behavior.

Theological semiotics is not only a study of the signs by which God's existence may be revealed to us, but a study of the signifying practices by which theological ideas may be expressed. While semiotic theology places its emphasis on theology, theological semiotics is more concerned with the nature of theological signs and with their primary modes of signifying. The kinds of signs with which theological semiotics is concerned include signs of God's power, signs of God's presence in the world, signs of God's blessing, signs of divine providence, signs of God's wisdom, signs of God's love, signs of Christ's glory, and other kinds of sacred or divine signs. Thus, Christian faith may be described by semiotic analysis as a structured system of sacred, divine, or theological signs.

The Christian Church may be described as a sign of God, insofar as the Church is the body of Christ. There are many members of the Church, but there is only one body, a universal body. We are all baptized by the Holy Spirit into the same body (1 Cor. 12:12-13), and thus we all belong to the same Church (although it may have many different names). Christ dwells in all of us, and we dwell in him.

To live in Christ is to dedicate oneself to following his example, and it is to reenact his journey through life, death, and resurrection. This reenactment of Christ's earthly and physical journey may signify our redemption from sin, through his sacrifice for us.

To live in Christ is thus to live in his body and blood. If we live in Christ, then the earthly lives that we lead are lived through faith in him (Gal. 2:20). For he gave his life so that we might be saved from our sins.

If we commit ourselves to Christ, then with God's grace, we will act righteously and justly. For righteousness is attained through faith (Romans 3:22). If we have faith in Christ, then by the grace of God, our faith will justify us, through the redemption that is in Christ Jesus (Romans 3:24).

Chapter I

THE SIGN AS SACRED

The Living Word

The Gospel According to Matthew (chapter 4:1-11) tells the story of Jesus going out into the wilderness and being tempted by the devil. The devil tells Jesus, "If you are the Son of God, command these stones to become loaves of bread." But Jesus answers, "It is written, man shall not live by bread alone, but by every word that proceeds from the mouth of God." Thus, the Gospel teaches that the Word of God provides a spiritual sustenance which is as important to our well-being as physical sustenance. We need more than physical sustenance in order to maintain our well-being; we need spiritual sustenance as well. Human existence is not only a physical reality, it is also a spiritual reality. The material and spiritual aspects of our existence are inseparable, and in order to reconcile them successfully we must consider both in judging the rightness or wrongness of our actions. In some cases, we may have to look beyond our physical needs and may have to consider our spiritual needs in order to perform the morally right action or the best action that we are capable of performing. In some cases, moreover, we may have to look beyond our own needs and may have to consider the needs of others in order to perform the right action. In any case, we can find spiritual support if we listen to and are guided by the Word of God.

The Word of God is literally a divine language. But "Word" here has a figurative meaning, because it also means law or *logos*. The Word of God is divine law, and as such it is absolute. It is universal and eternal, as distinguished from human law. It is the law that sustains not only our being in the world but also the being of all living things and the being of the whole universe. As divine law, however, it must be recognized and interpreted if it is to be taken as a source of guidance for the actions of human beings. Thus, errors in recognition or interpretation of the Word of God may lead individuals to perform actions that are misguided.

The "Word" of God proceeds from the "mouth" of God, and it is therefore articulated. At the same time, however, it is not merely spoken or written, it is living Word. It is "the Word made flesh." John (1:14) says, "And the Word became flesh and dwelt among us, full of grace and truth; we have beheld his glory, glory as of the only Son from the Father." Thus, Jesus is the same as the Word of God, and he is identified with divine law, divine grace, and divine truth. The word "Jesus" is a name that can be spoken or written, but Jesus is also the Word, which as divine law is the absolute ground of all meaning and signification.

Jesus as Symbol of God

Jesus is a symbol of divine love and compassion. "For God so loved the world that he gave his only Son, that whoever believes in him should not perish but have eternal life" (John 3:16). Jesus is the embodiment of God's presence in the world. In Jesus, physical reality and spiritual reality are one and the same. Jesus is also a symbol of moral and spiritual perfection. His death and resurrection are symbolic of the triumph over suffering that is possible for those who have faith in God. He is a symbol who may himself be symbolized by various titles (such as "the Lord" and "the King of Kings"), by iconic images in art, and by physical objects (such as a wafer and a cup of wine, a crucifix above an altar, or a plastic ornament on the dashboard of a car).

In the scriptures, Jesus is referred to by various symbolic names and expressions, such as "the Son of God," "the Son of man," "the Redeemer," "the Lamb of God," and "the Messiah." Similarly, God is referred to by various names, such as "the heavenly Father," "the Almighty," and "the Lord Jehovah." Thus, the name "God" is a symbol for a supreme being or for an ultimate reality. The name "God" connotes an absolute being that is all-powerful and all-knowing, a being that surpasses the limits of our understanding.

According to John (1:1), "In the beginning was the Word, and the Word was with God, and the Word was God." The being of the Word is thus inseparable from the being of God. Word and God are One. But "Word" here has a symbolic meaning; it does not refer to an element of speech or writing, but to the law on which all being (including the being of speech and writing) depends. The name "Word" is a symbol for divine law, but divine law is the principle on which all symbolization depends. The Word as law thus governs the origins of the signs and symbols that may be used to refer to God. However, the phrase "Word of God" also has a literal meaning which contributes to its symbolic meaning. Even if God as Word transcends the limits of language and cannot be adequately described by mere words, the phrase "Word of God" may signify our need to think of God symbolically and our need to use language as a vehicle of religious expression.

Christianity as a Mode of Language

Christianity can therefore be described not only as a religious faith, but as a symbolic language by which this faith reveals and expresses itself. As a mode of language, Christianity has its own vocabulary and syntactical rules. It has its own ethical and practical rules, i.e. rules that govern the uses, purposes, and effects of its signs. Thus, it may be a conventional language as well as a sacred language. However, it is a language of faith and not merely a language of belief.

Christian semiotics is therefore a metalanguage about Christianity. Christianity may be a language in which the Word of God is revealed through the teachings of Jesus Christ.

Christians are members of a religious community who share a language of faith. In this sense, they are also members of a linguistic community. To belong to a religious community is, in some way, to share a language of faith with other members of that community. To the extent that members of various religious communities share the same understanding of signs and symbols, they may be able to communicate effectively. Christianity may be only one of many religious faiths (or religious languages) in a culture or society.

This is not to equate faith and language. Faith may be expressed non-linguistically as well as linguistically. However, in order to talk about faith, we must employ signs and symbols as instruments of language.

We may also have a fundamental need as human beings to conceptualize our experience symbolically. Thus, Christianity is not only a way of thinking symbolically; it is a way of acting and communicating symbolically.

Christianity may be described as a semiotic system, i.e. as a system of signs and symbols. Christian semiotics may involve the study of various signifying (or discursive) practices by which signs and symbols of religious faith are produced and interpreted.

The question arises as to whether an investigation of Christian semiotics is actually an investigation of the teachings of Christianity or whether it is merely an investigation of the principles of semiotics. The viewpoint adopted here is that the teachings of Christianity are so closely connected with symbolic modes of expression that in order to fully investigate the meaning of those teachings we must recognize their signification as signs of faith.

At the same time, Christian semiotics cannot be merely a sociolinguistic method of inquiry, because the symbols that it studies refer to something that surpasses the power of words to express, and they represent something that transcends the limits of language.

The concept of Christianity as a mode of language is also a metaphor for the way in which religious faith can enable us to express our feelings of love and compassion for each other. Metaphorically, the various denominations and traditions within the Christian Church may all be "dialects" (cultural, ethnic, geographical) of a single language.

The Word as the Light of the World

The importance of language as a structural principle of society is seen in the story of the tower of Babel in the Book of Genesis (Chapter 11). According to this story, all peoples of the earth originally spoke one language. They attempted to "make a name for themselves" by building a tower that would reach heaven. This was an attempt by them to rival the greatness of God, and God punished them for their arrogance by confusing their language, so that they no longer understood each other's speech. They were then scattered across the face of the earth, unable to communicate with each other. Thus, the tower of Babel was a symbol of human pride and arrogance. Language as a means of social and religious expression was revealed to be something that could be given to us by God. The estrangement of human beings from each other because of their differences in language reflected their estrangement from God because of their acts of disobedience to divine law. According to this biblical story, language as a principle of order has always been necessary in order for social harmony and well-being to be attained.

Another interpretation of the story is that God punished the people for building the tower of Babel because they had not sought his grace, and because they had decided that they were strong enough to act independently of him. Another interpretation of the story is that God punished the people for their disobedience to his command that they spread across the earth (Gen. 9:1). Another interpretation is that the people were punished because they had decided to build the tower not to glorify God, but to make a name for themselves.

The importance of God's Word as a source of guidance is indicated by Psalm 119, verse 105: "Your word is a lamp to my feet and a light to my path." The Word of God is a light that illuminates the darkness of the world. Thus, Jesus says to Paul, "I send you to open their eyes, that they may turn from darkness to light and from the power of Satan to God, that they may receive forgiveness of sins and a place among those who are sanctified by faith in me" (Acts 26:17-18). Light is symbolic of obedience to God's will, and darkness is symbolic of ignorance or disobedience. Thus, Jesus says to the crowd of listeners, as he delivers his Sermon on the Mount, "You are the light of the world. A city set on a hill cannot be hid. Nor do men light a lamp and put it under a bushel, but on a stand, and it gives light to all in the house. Let your light so shine before men, that they may see your good works and give glory to your Father who is in heaven" (Matthew 5: 14-16).

In Exodus 3:4, God speaks to Moses through the burning bush. In Genesis 12, God speaks to Abraham.

Jesus teaches us that if we wish to be guided by the spirit of truth, then we must obey the Word of God. He says, "If anyone loves me, he will keep my word, and my Father will love him and make our home with him. He who does not love me does not keep my words; and the word which you hear is not mine but the Father's who sent me" (John 14:23-24).

Christian Symbolism

Symbols of Christian faith include the cross, the sacraments, the bread and wine that are served at holy communion, the chalice, the prayer book, the act of making the sign of the cross with one's hand, the act of genuflecting before an altar, the rites of Ash Wednesday, the rite of Christian burial, the confession of sins, and the Lord's Prayer. The offering of money to the church during a service of worship is a symbol of thanksgiving. The saying of a blessing before meals is a symbolic act, and the celebration of Christian festival days such as Christmas and Easter also has symbolic connotations. The collar which a priest wears is a symbolic clerical garment. Services of worship and liturgical rites are symbolic expressions of faith. In Christian iconography, the descending dove is a symbol of the Holy Spirit, and the fish symbol represents Christ.

Liturgical colors used for vestments and for church decorations symbolize the various seasons of the Church year. They include purple (symbolizing penitence) during Advent and Lent, white or gold (symbolizing purity, holiness, joy, and triumph) during the Christmas and Easter seasons, black (symbolizing mourning) on Good Friday, red (symbolizing blood and Christ's death on the cross, but also symbolizing fire and the Holy Spirit) during Holy Week and at Pentecost, and green (symbolizing growth and regeneration) during the season from Pentecost to Advent.

The various configurations of the cross have symbolic connotations. For example, an X-shaped cross (or saltire) is symbolic of Saint Andrew, who is said to have asked his executioners to use a different kind of cross than that on which Christ was crucified, as he considered himself unworthy of being crucified on the same kind of cross as Christ.[1] The shape of the Greek cross (having arms of equal length) was used as a floor plan in Byzantine church architecture (in which the

---

1. Rowena and Rupert Shepherd, *1000 Symbols* (New York: Thames & Hudson, 2002) p. 337.

altar was placed at the center of the church). The Calvary cross mounted on three steps symbolizes the crucifixion on Mount Golgatha.

Number symbolism is found throughout the bible. The number "one" is symbolic of unity and beginning. The number "two" is symbolic of division and separation. The number "three" is symbolic of God, Son, and the Holy Spirit.

The number "seven" in the bible represents completeness and perfection. For example, God rested on the seventh day after creating the world (Gen. 2:2). God told Noah to take seven pairs of all animals, male and female, onto the ark (Gen.7:2). The people of Israel observed the feast of booths for seven days, starting on the fifteenth day of the seventh month (Lev. 23:33-34). The Lord told Joshua that seven priests would bear seven trumpets before the ark of the covenant, and he told Joshua to march around the city of Jericho seven times (Joshua 4:4-5). Jesus told Peter that he should forgive his brother not seven times, but seventy times seven (Matt. 18:22). The Book of Revelation mentions seven churches (1:4), seven golden lampstands (1:12), seven spirits of God (3:1), seven stars (3:1), seven torches of fire (4:5), seven seals (5:5), seven angels (8:2), and seven trumpets (8:2).

The number "forty" also appears frequently in the bible, standing for trial and preparation. For example, God told Noah that it would rain for forty days and nights (Gen. 7:4). Moses was on Mount Sinai for forty days and nights (Ex. 24:18). God told Moses and Aaron that the people of Israel would wander in the wilderness for forty years (Num. 14:33). Elijah lived for forty days and nights without food after he had eaten bread given to him by an angel (1 Kings 19:8). Jesus fasted forty days and nights in the wilderness (Matt. 4:2). Jesus remained with his disciples for forty days after his resurrection (Acts 1:3).

Rosary symbolism is another form of Christian symbolism, based on devotional prayer and on meditation concerning the mysteries of redemption. The rosary includes the recitation of sequences of prayers while a set of beads is used to count the prayers and while the mysteries of redemption are reflected on.

Each sequence of prayers in the rosary includes the recitation of the Lord's Prayer, ten "Hail Marys,"[2] and the "Glory be to the Father" prayer,[3] while the mysteries are sequentially announced and reflected on. Each decade or sequence of "Hail Marys" corresponds to a joyful mystery, a luminous mystery, a sorrowful

---

2. "Hail Mary, full of grace, the Lord is with thee, blessed art thou among women, and blessed is the fruit of thy womb, Jesus. Holy Mary, Mother of God, pray for us sinners, now and at the hour of our death. Amen."
3. "Glory be to the Father, and to the Son, and to the Holy Spirit. As it was in the beginning, is now, and ever shall be, world without end. Amen."

mystery, or a glorious mystery. There are five joyful mysteries, five luminous mysteries, five sorrowful mysteries, and five glorious mysteries. Thus, a complete rosary involving one of the four sets of mysteries usually includes fifty "Hail Marys" (corresponding to fifty beads).

The joyful mysteries are 1) the annunciation, 2) the visitation, 3) the nativity, 4) the presentation of Jesus at the temple, and 5) the finding of Jesus in the temple.

The luminous mysteries are 1) the baptism of Jesus, 2) the marriage at Cana, 3) the proclamation of the kingdom of God, 4) the transfiguration, and 5) the institution of the eucharist.

The sorrowful mysteries are 1) the agony in the garden, 2) the scourging at the pillar, 3) the crowning with thorns, 4) the carrying of the cross, and 5) the crucifixion.

The glorious mysteries are 1) the resurrection, 2) the ascension, 3) the descent of the Holy Spirit, 4) the assumption, and 5) the coronation of the Blessed Virgin Mary.

The Stations of the Cross are a series of scenes from Christ's Passion which symbolize his suffering on the cross. They are 1) Jesus is condemned to death, 2) Jesus is given the cross to carry, 3) he falls for the first time, 4) he meets his mother, 5) Simon of Cyrene helps Jesus to carry the cross, 6) Saint Veronica wipes Jesus' face, 7) Jesus falls a second time, 8) he tells the women of Jerusalem not to weep for him, 9) he falls a third time, 10), he is stripped of his clothing, 11) he is nailed to the cross, 12) he dies on the cross, 13) his body is taken down from the cross, and 14) he is laid in the tomb. Each of the Stations of the Cross can be a subject of devotional prayer and meditation.

A nun's ring symbolizes that she is married to Christ. A bishop's crozier (pastoral staff) signifies that he is shepherd of the flock of God.

The traditional Gothic-style habit (or ensemble of clothing) worn by a nun has many symbolic meanings. A traditional habit may include 1) a *coif* (a close-fitting headcap covering the ears and worn under the veil) 2) a *bandeau* (a white headband worn across the forehead), 3) a *veil*, 4) a *wimple* or *guimpe* (pronounced "gimp," a starched bib or folded cloth worn around the neck), 5) a *tunic* (a robe with long sleeves), 6) a *scapular* (a long apron-like garment worn over the tunic), 7) a *cincture* (a belt worn around the waist of the tunic), and 8) a *cappa* (a cape worn over the tunic).

A nun's habit may signify that she is not only shrouded from the world but shrouded as an individual.[4] It also signifies that she is protected by Christ. It also signifies her spirituality and her commitment to Christ. The veil, which is colored white on the inside and black on the outside, signifies her chastity and her being "dead to the world." The coif signifies that she keeps closely in mind the presence of a heavenly reality. The cincture tied in three knots symbolizes her vows of poverty, chastity, and obedience. The scapular signifies the yoke of Christ.

The garments worn by a priest may include a *cassock* (a tunic with long sleeves) or an *alb* (a white linen vestment with long sleeves). A cassock may be combined with a *surplice* and a *stole*, or an alb may be combined with a stole and a *chasuble*. A surplice is a loose-fitting, broad-sleeved tunic worn over the cassock, a stole is a long narrow strip of cloth worn around the neck, a cincture is a belt worn around the waist of a cassock or alb, and a chasuble is a sleeveless outer vestment worn by the celebrant at Mass. Deacons wear a stole draped over the left shoulder, while priests wear a stole draped around the neck. The stole is symbolic of the yoke of Christ.

In the Roman Catholic Church, the color of a cassock may signify rank in the priesthood (i.e. black for priests, purple for bishops, red for cardinals, and white for the pope).[5] In the Anglican Church, bishops may wear either black or purple cassocks.

A Roman cassock typically has thirty-three buttons, symbolizing the years of the life of Jesus.

Symbols of Christmas include Christmas trees, Christmas cards, wreaths, candles, Christmas cards, and scenes of the nativity.

Easter symbols include Easter eggs (symbolizing new life and rebirth), the Easter bunny (symbolizing fertility and regeneration), Easter baskets, the Easter bonnet (signifying celebration), and the Easter lilly (symbolizing new life, rebirth, grace, and beauty).

The sign "INRI" is another kind of Christian symbol. It may be found on a crucifix above the figure of Jesus, and it stands for what Pilate wrote on the sign that was placed above Jesus on the cross (John 19:19): *Iesus Nazarenus Rex Iudaeorum* (*Jesus of Nazareth, King of the Jews*).

Another Christian symbol is the "chi-rho" monogram or "Christogram," consisting of an X superimposed on a P, standing for the first two Greek letters of Christ's name (Χριστος, *Christos*, Χ = chi, Ρ = rho). It is often embroidered onto altar cloths and onto vestments such as stoles and chasubles.

---

4. Elizabeth Kuhns, *The Habit: A History of the Clothing of Catholic Nuns* (New York: Doubleday, 2003), p. 7.
5. *Ibid.*, p. 188.

The IHS monogram signifies the first three letters of Jesus' name in Greek (Ἰησους, *Iesous*, Ι = iota, η = eta, ς = sigma). The monogram is sometimes stamped onto communion wafers or is embroided onto the backs of chasubles. The Jesuit emblem has the letters IHS, surrounded by rays of sunlight, representing the glory of Christ. The letters are also sometimes said to be an acronym for the Latin phrase, *Iesous Hominum Salvator* (*Jesus, savior of man*).

Luther's seal is a well-known symbol of the Lutheran faith. It has a black cross in a red heart, signifying that faith in Christ is a source of joy, comfort, and peace. The heart is in the center of a white rose, mounted on a sky-blue background encircled by a golden ring, symbolizing eternal blessedness and heavenly joy.

The cross and flame symbol of the United Methodist Church, officially adopted in 1968, has a cross, representing Christ's sacrifice, and a double flame, representing the Holy Spirit.

The symbol of the Church of England has a cross encompassed by a circular "e."

The shield of the U.S. Episcopal Church, adopted as an official symbol in 1940, has a red cross on a white background, which together symbolize the Church of England, to which the Episcopal Church is linked as a member of the Anglican Communion. In the upper left corner of the shield is a blue quadrant, in which nine small crosses are arranged in an X-shaped (saltire) pattern. The nine crosses represent the original nine dioceses of the American Episcopal Church, and the saltire pattern is a reminder of the Episcopal Church of Scotland, which consecrated the first American bishop, Samuel Seabury, in 1784. The red, white, and blue colors of the shield also represent the colors of the American flag.

The seal of the U.S. Presbyterian Church shows a cross with flames on either side, symbolizing the Holy Spirit. The upper portion of the cross is shaped like a descending dove, and the horizontal section of the cross is shaped like an open book, representing the scriptures.

Candles are often used in Christian churches, and they may signify the light of God and the flame of the Holy Spirit.

The Theology of Signs

In the Bible, miracles are described as signs of God's power. For example, in Exodus Chapter 4, God tells Moses to cast his rod upon the ground, whereupon it turns into a serpent. God then changes the serpent back into a rod that Moses can hold in his hand. God then tells Moses to put his hand to his bosom, whereupon Moses' hand is infected with leprosy. God then tells Moses again to put his hand to his bosom, whereupon Moses' hand is restored to health. God then says to Moses, "If they will not believe you or heed the first sign, they may believe the latter sign. If they will not believe even these two signs or heed your voice, you shall take some water from the Nile and pour it upon the dry ground; and the water which you shall take from the Nile will become blood upon the dry ground" (4:8-9).

In Exodus Chapter 3, the angel of the Lord appears to Moses as a flame of fire in the midst of a bush. Moses is amazed, because the bush is burning without being consumed. The burning bush is thus a symbol of divine revelation.

In Genesis Chapter 17, circumcision is described as a sign of the covenant between God and Abraham. In Exodus Chapter 12, God tells Moses and Aaron that lamb's blood should be placed as a sign at the door of every household belonging to the congregation of Israel, so that the people of Israel will be spared when death strikes the first-born of every family in the land of the Pharoah (1-13).

The names of many biblical figures have symbolic meanings. For example, God changes Abram's name to *Abraham*, which means "father of a great multitude" (Gen. 17:5). The name *Daniel* in Hebrew means "God is my judge." The name *Peter* is derived from the Greek name *Petros* (πετρος), meaning "stone." Thus, Simon is given the name *Peter* by Jesus, who tells him that he is the rock upon whom the church will be built (Matt.16:18).

The name *Jesus* in Hebrew means "God saves." The name *Christ* is derived from the Greek word *Christos* (χριστός), meaning *the Messiah*, i.e. "the anointed one." The name *Emmanuel* in Hebrew means "God with us." Thus, Joseph is told by an angel in a dream that his wife Mary will bear a child who will be named "Jesus" and who will also be called "Emmanuel" (Matt. 1:21-23).

Other biblical names include *Abigail* (which in Hebrew means "God is joy"), *Ann* (which in Hebrew means "gracious"), *Benjamin* ("son of my right hand"), *David* ("beloved"), *Elijah* ("the Lord is my God"), *Isaiah* ("God is salvation"), *Ishmael* ("God will hear"), *Israel* ("prince of God"), *Jeremiah* ("God has uplifted"), *Jonathan* ("gift of God"), *Judah* ("praised"), *Malachi* ("my messenger, my angel"), *Rebecca* ("servant of God"), *Reuben* ("behold, a son"), *Sarah* ("lady" or "princess"), and *Zachariah* ("remembered by the Lord").

At the Last Supper, Jesus sits at a table with his twelve disciples, and he gives them bread, saying "Take, eat; this is my body." Then he takes a cup of wine, and he gives it to them, saying "Drink of it, all of you; for this is my blood of the covenant, which is poured out for many for the forgiveness of sins" (Matt. 26:26-28). The bread and wine may or may not be literally his body and blood (depending on one's interpretation of the scriptures), but they are iconic in their resemblance to flesh and blood They represent the spiritual sustenance that Christ provides to all who believe in him. Thus, Christ says, "I am the bread of life; he who comes to me shall not hunger, and he who believes in me shall never thirst" (John 6:35).

A sacrament is traditionally defined as an outward and visible sign of an inward and spiritual grace. Saint Augustine of Hippo (354-430) described it as a sacred sign (i.e. a sign of the sacred). It may thus be a physical reality that signifies a spiritual reality. It may be accessible to sensory experience, while the divine grace that it signifies may transcend sensory experience.

The words that are spoken and the acts that are performed during the administration of a sacrament are signifiers (sign-vehicles) of the sacrament, and the sacrament itself is a signifier of God's grace. The signification of the sacrament depends not only on the sign-vehicles that are used to convey it, but also on the sacred thing to which they refer. The signifying practice (the administration of the sacrament) bestows a benefit on the receiver to whom the sign-vehicles are addressed, because the receiver, through the process by which the sign-vehicles function as a sign, is able to recognize the meaning of the sacrament, i.e. that all human beings, regardless of their past sins, are eligible for God's grace if they repent and ask for forgiveness.

God's gift of grace is a mystery which is revealed to us through the sacraments. God loves us, regardless of whether we deserve it or not. All of the sacraments of the Church are symbols of God's grace. Thus, they reassure us that despite our faults and misdeeds, God will always love us and that if we truly repent of our sins, God will forgive us. The sacraments not only convey grace and reassure us of God's love, but also strengthen our faith and renew our sense of commitment to the Church and to each other.

Chapter II

THE SIGNIFIER AND THE SIGNIFIED

The Theory of the Linguistic Sign

Saussure

Ferdinand de Saussure (1916), in his teachings on linguistics, makes a basic distinction between language (*langue*) and the activity of speaking (*parole*). He says that speaking may be performed by an individual but that language is the social expression of speech. Language is a system of signs which evolves from the activity of speech.

According to Saussure, language is a link between thought and sound, and it is a means of expressing thoughts by using sound-images to represent them. In every linguistic sign, a sound-image is used to represent an idea or concept. A sound-image is a signifier of a signified idea. The connection between a signifier and the idea which it signifies is arbitrary, because any signifier may conceivably be used to represent any given idea or concept.

Thus, Saussure describes language as a structured system of arbitrary signs, and he calls the study of signs "semiology." Signs are arbitrary, because the choice of any given signifier to represent a particular concept is "unmotivated" by any natural connection between the signifier and the signified concept. The connection between the signifier and the signified is merely conventional. However, symbols differ from signs in not being wholly arbitrary and in having a rational relationship with their signified concepts.

Saussure's distinction between signs and symbols may be faulty in several respects. As an example of the "natural" connection between a symbol and its signified concept, he says that the symbol of justice, a pair of scales, is not arbitrary, because it could not be replaced by merely any symbol, such as a chariot.[1] However, the symbol of a pair of scales is an example of what Charles S. Peirce (1903) would define as an "icon" (a sign which resembles its object). Symbols do not have to resemble the objects that they signify, any more than other signs have to resemble the objects they signify. The connection between a symbol and its object may be just as much a matter of convention as the connection between any other sign and its object. Moreover, Saussure suggests that a "natural" connection between a symbol and its signified concept is also a rational or logical connection, and he thus confuses the "natural" nature of a symbol with its rationality.

---

1. Ferdinand de Saussure, *Course in General Linguistics*, edited by Charles Bally and Albert Sechehaye in collaboration with Albert Riedlinger, translated by Wade Baskin. (New York: McGraw-Hill Book Company, 1966), p. 68.

According to Saussure, relations between signs may be either syntagmatic or associative (paradigmatic). Syntagmatic relations are linear, sequential, or successive, while paradigmatic relations are non-linear, substitutive, or synchronous. Syntagmatic and paradigmatic relations each generate their own sets of values. Thus, structural analysis of a language enables us to study it as a system of values. The linguistic value of a signifier may be determined by its ability to represent a signified concept. The value of a concept may be determined by its relation to other concepts.

Peirce

Charles S. Peirce's (1903) theory of signs asserts that all modes of thinking depend on the use of signs. Every thought is a sign, and every act of reasoning consists of the interpretation of signs. Signs function as mediators between the external world of physical objects and the internal world of ideas. Signs are mental representations of objects, and objects are known by perception of their signs. Thus, "semiosis" is the process by which representations of objects function as signs. Semiosis is a process of cooperation between signs, their objects, and their "interpretants" (mental representations). "Semiotic" is the study of semiosis, and it is an inquiry into the conditions which are necessary in order for representations of objects to function as signs.

According to Peirce, "meaning" is a triadic relation between a sign, an object, and an interpretant. This triadic relation is not reducible to a set of dyadic relations between a sign and an object or between an object and an interpretant. Meaning is never reducible to Firstness or Secondness, and it can only be a "genuine" Thirdness. Firstness is the mode of being of that which is without reference to any subject or object. Secondness is the mode of being of that which is itself in referring to a second object, regardless of any third subject. Thirdness is the mode of being of that which is itself in bringing a second and a third subject into relation with each other.[2] Thirdness brings Firstness and Secondness into relation with each other, and it mediates between them. Thirdness is the mode of being of signs, insofar as signs mediate relations between their objects and their interpretants.

Peirce defines a sign (or representamen) as anything that denotes an object, and he defines an object as anything that can be thought. A sign may be an icon,

---

2. Charles Sanders Peirce, *Collected Papers of Charles Sanders Peirce, Volume I*, paragraph 191, 1903 (Cambridge: Harvard University Press, 1960), p. 79.

an index, or a symbol, depending on its relation to its "dynamical object" (the object that actually causes the sign). An icon (such as a picture, image, model, or diagram) resembles its dynamical object, an index (such as a clock, thermometer, fuel gauge, or medical symptom) demonstrates the influence of its dynamical object, and a symbol (such as a trophy, medal, receipt, diploma, monument, word, phrase, or sentence) refers to its dynamical object.

Peirce defines a "token" as an actually existing thing or event that acts as a sign, and he defines a "type" as a legisign (a law that acts as a sign). Symbols may be laws or types, and they may act through tokens. Tokens are replicas (individual examples) of symbols and legisigns. Types may be replicated (instantiated) by tokens, and tokens may be motivated by types.

If every thought is a sign, then every thought may be described as an icon, an index, or a symbol. Icons and indices may be constituents of symbols. Symbols may be laws or general "types" (i.e. legisigns), and they may be general terms that are used to produce concepts. Symbols may also be conventional signs that are used to signify other signs.

Signs may vary in their degree of iconicity. Pure icons are indistinguishable from the objects they represent. Thus, the actual icons with which semiotics is concerned are described by Peirce as "hypoicons." Hypoicons include images (whose mode of Firstness is a First), diagrams (whose mode of Firstness is a Second), and metaphors (whose mode of Firstness is a Third).

Icons may in some cases be very concrete in their signification, while symbols may in some cases be very abstract in their signification. Concrete symbols may be more "iconic" than abstract symbols. However, iconicity may be either "natural" or "conventional" (i.e. the iconicity of some signs may be a matter of convention rather than a matter of natural resemblance). Peirce regards iconicity as a matter of natural resemblance, and thus he defines signs whose iconicity is a matter of convention as "symbols." Symbols that resemble their objects are "iconic legisigns."

Morris

Charles W. Morris (1971) divides semiotics into three interrelated sciences or disciplines: 1) syntactics (the study of the methods by which signs may be combined to form compound signs), 2) semantics (the study of the signification of signs), and 3) pragmatics (the study of the origins, uses, and effects of signs). While the syntactic dimension of semiosis is governed by the relations which signs have to each other, the semantic dimension is governed by the relations which signs have to the objects or events that they signify, and the pragmatic dimension is governed by the relations which signs have to their producers and interpreters.

According to Morris, there are four components of semiosis (the process by which sign-vehicles function as signs): 1) the *sign-vehicle* (the object or event which functions as a sign), 2) the *designatum* (the kind of object or class of objects which the sign designates), 3) the *interpretant* (the disposition of an interpreter to initiate a response-sequence as a result of perceiving the sign), and 4) the *interpreter* (the person for whom the sign-vehicle functions as a sign). Every sign must have a *designatum*, but not every sign must have a *denotatum* (an actually existing object or event which is denoted by the sign). If a sign denotes something, then it has a *denotatum* as well as a *designatum*. If a sign does not denote anything, then it has a *designatum*, but it does not have any *denotata*. Another way of saying this is that a sign must "designate" something, but it does not have to "denote" anything.[3]

All signs are signals or symbols, says Morris. Signals are not interpreted to signify other signs, but symbols are interpreted to signify other signs. Symbols may be used as substitutes for synonymous signs, but signals are not used as substitutes for synonymous signs.

Morris defines the *significatum* (or signification) of a sign as the set of conditions under which the sign denotes something.[4] If a sign denotes something, then the response-sequences to which the interpreter is disposed by perceiving the sign may be completed by the interpreter. Sign-vehicles which have the same *significata* belong to the same "sign-family." Each member of a sign-family may prepare the interpreter to initiate the same response-sequences to *denotata*, since each sign has the same signification.

A sign that has more than one signification may belong to more than one sign-family. The degree of synonymity between various signs or sign-families may be determined by the degree of similarity in their signification. Signs that are similar in their conditions of denotation are also similar in their *significata* (or in their signification).

According to Morris, a language is a system of simple and compound signs that have interpersonal and plurisituational signification (i.e. conditions of deno-

---

3. Charles Morris, *Writings on the General Theory of Signs* (The Hauge: Mouton, 1971), p. 416.
4. *Ibid.*, p. 144.

tation which are the same for many interpreters and which remain relatively constant from situation to situation).

Language-signs (or "lansigns") must include some "comsigns" (signs that have the same *significata* for producers as for interpreters).[5] Comsigns may be divided into two kinds: 1) "comsignals," which do not act as substitutes for other comsigns, and 2) "comsymbols," which act as substitutes for other comsigns.[6] Comsigns may vary in the extent to which their significata are the same for their interpreters as for their producers.

Morris avoids using the term "meaning" as a synonym for signification, because he says that "meaning" is an ambiguous term and that it may be used to refer to *designata, denotata, interpretants,* or *significata*.[7] Various sign-processes may constitute the "meaning" of signs, and thus it may be preferable to use more specific terms in order to define the components of semiosis.

Langer

Susanne K. Langer (1942) explains that signs *indicate* things, but that symbols *represent* things. While a sign announces its object (or referent) to an interpreter, a symbol is a vehicle by which the interpreter can conceive of the object. More than one symbol may represent the same object, and each symbol may give rise to a plurality of conceptions. Signification is a function of signs, but denotation and connotation are functions of symbols. Signification is a direct relation between a sign and an object, but denotation is a complex relationship that includes a symbol, an object, an interpreter, and a conception (connotation) of the object that the symbol conveys. Thus, the meaning of symbols may be denotative or connotative, literal or figurative, discursive or non-discursive (presentational).

Symbolization is essential to conceptual thinking, says Langer. We cannot think conceptually without using symbols to represent our thoughts. Concepts are abstract symbolic forms which are embodied as "conceptions" in every act of discursive thought. Every act of reasoning involves the manipulation of symbols. All language is characterized by discursiveness, and all discourse has at least two elements: 1) the context (the verbal or practical setting in which it appears), and 2) the "novelty" (the thought which the speaker is trying to express).[8] The con-

---

5. *Ibid.*, p. 113.
6. *Ibid.*, p. 361.
7. *Ibid.*, p. 55.
8. Susanne K. Langer, *Philosophy in a New Key: A Study in the Symbolism of Reason, Rite, and Art* (Cambridge: Harvard University Press, 1942), p. 139.

text indicates whether the meaning of an expression is literal or figurative, and if the latter is the case, then the context also indicates how this meaning is to be interpreted.[9]

Langer distinguishes between discursive and non-discursive (presentational) symbolism by saying that discursive symbols may be linear or successive, while non-discursive symbols may be nonlinear and presented simultaneously. Presentational symbols may have innumerable combinations, and they may include qualities, rhythms, lines, colors, and sounds. Thus, non-discursive formulations may give rise to modes of symbolism that cannot be subjected to the syntactic or grammatical rules of language.

Langer describes music, art, and ritual as modes of symbolism whose meaning may not be translatable into words. They may be formulations of emotions that language cannot articulate. Literal or connotative meaning may not be assignable to their structures in the same way that it is assignable to linguistic structures.

Whitehead

Alfred North Whitehead (1927) refers to the nexus or system of relations between symbols and meanings as a mode of perception called "symbolic reference." Symbolic reference is a mixed mode of perception, which is characterized by an interplay between two primary modes of perception, presentational immediacy and causal efficacy. Presentational immediacy is a direct perception of present "actual occasions," while causal efficacy is a direct perception of prior actual occacions which are causally related to subsequent actual occasions. The pure mode of presentatonal immediacy gives no information about the past or future, but if it is combined with causal efficacy, it may enable present and past actual occasions to be unified. Actual entities (or occasions) which are perceived in the mode of presentational immediacy may give information about physical or conceptual objects in the mode of causal efficacy, and physical or conceptual objects which are perceived in the mode of causal efficacy may give information about actual entitites (or occasions) in the mode of presentational immediacy.

According to Whitehead, symbolic reference between the modes of causal efficacy and presntational immediacy occurs when perception in the mode of efficacy evokes its correlate in the mode of immediacy, or vice versa. In order for this interplay to occur, there must be a "presented locus" which is a datum for both modes of perception. The presented locus is a common ground for both causal

---

9. *Ibid.*, p. 140.

efficacy and presentational immediacy. It is directly perceived by presentional immediacy, but it is indirectly perceived by causal efficacy.

Hjelmslev

Another theory of sign function is provided by the linguist Louis Hjemlslev (1943), who defines a sign as a linguistic unit consisting of an "expression-form" and a "content form," which are correlated to each other . The interdependence between the expression and content of a sign thus establishes a sign-function. Every sign has both an expression-form and a content-form. Expression and content are the two "functives" (terminals) of every sign-function.

Hjelmslev says that semiotics is a study of signs that is analgous to a language and that may therefore be studied by a "metasemiotic." A metasemiotic is a metalanguage that is concerned with the terminology of semiotics. Hjelmslev also makes a distinction between scientific and non-scientific semiotics, and he defines "semiology" as the study of non-scientific semiotics. A "metasemiology" is a scientific metasemiotic that studies the terminology of semiology.[10]

Eco

Umberto Eco (1976) agrees with Hjelmslev that every sign belongs to at least one content-plane that is conventionally correlated to an expression-plane. A sign cannot belong to an expression-plane without belonging to a content-plane, and it cannot belong to a content-plane without belonging to an expression plane. However, a sign may in some cases belong to more than one expression-plane and to more than one content-plane. The content of a sign may have more than one expression, and the expression of a sign may have more than one content. Thus, semiotic codes are necessary in order to correlate the expression of signs to their content. Codes are correlational devices that are used to generate sign-functions.[11]

Eco explains that a system of signification (or "s-code") may include syntactic rules (which are rules for the combination of signs), semantic rules (which are rules for the signification of signs), and behavioral rules (which are rules for the

---

10. Louis Hjelmslev, *Prolegomena to a Theory of Language* (Madision: University of Wisconsin Press, 1963), p. 120.
11. Umberto Eco, *A Theory of Semiotics* (Bloomington: Indiana University Press, 1976), p. 48.

coordination of syntactic and semantic rules, so that proper understanding of a given array of signs can produce a corresponding behavioral response). Thus, an "s-code" is a system of rules which has syntactic, semantic, and behavioral components. It differs from an ordinary code in being a system of signification, while an ordinary code is merely a correlational device for producing or interpreting signs. An ordinary code may correlate the items of different information systems or the items of different "s-codes."

According to Eco, the content and not the referent of a sign is the location of its meaning. The meaning of a sign is a "cultural unit," because the meaning of every sign is culturally defined. A cultural unit may be defined as a semantic unit (a content unit or "sememe"), because it may be analyzed into its elementary semantic components (its "semes" or semantic markers). A cultural unit may also be defined as a syntactic unit (an expression unit or "lexeme"), because it may be analyzed into its elementary syntactic components (its syntactic markers).[12]

A sign-function may be denotative to the extent that its expression does not signify the content of another sign-function, but it may be connotative to the extent that its expression signifies the content of another sign-function. To denote is to signify something without relying on a preceding denotation, but to connote is to rely on a preceding denotation in order to signify something.

Eco distinguishes between "types" and "tokens" as signs that have different modes of production. A type is an abstract model for a concrete token, and a token is an actual sign-vehicle that is used for communication. A token is also an individual occurrence of an expression, and it may signify either an "expression-type" or a "content-type." An expression-type is an element of an expression-plane, while a content-type is an element of a content-plane.

According to Eco, the modes of sign-production may be classified according to four criteria: 1) the amount of physical labor that is necessary in order to produce expressions, 2) the type-token ratio, 3) the continuum that is to be shaped, and 4) the mode and rate of articulation. These criteria may be used to describe both the modes of sign-production by which expressions are produced and the modes of sign-production by which expression-tokens are correlated to expression-types and content-types.

Eco rejects what he calls "naïve iconism" as a theory which falsely assumes that so-called "iconic" signs" must be similar or analogous to their referents, and he argues that the iconicity of any particular mode of sign-production is a matter of cultural convention. He explains, however, that to assert that the iconicity of any

---

12. *Ibid.*, p.72.

particular mode of sign-production is a matter of cultural convention is not to assert that it is a matter which is decided arbitrarily. To the contrary, the degree of iconicity of any particular expression may be determined by the degree to which the expression is correlated to its content, and it may not be determined by the degree to which the expression is similar or analogous to some object to which it may refer. Iconicity may therefore be a property of a particular mode of producing sign-functions, but it may be not be a property of any particular kind of sign.

Sebeok

Thomas Sebeok (1994) divides signs into six types: 1) symptoms, 2) signals, 3) icons, 4) indices, 5) symbols, and 6) names. A symptom is a natural sign of an altered state. A signal is a stimulus or trigger for a response. An icon is a sign which simulates or resembles its referent. An index is a sign which in one way or another is contiguous to its referent, indicating it or demonstrating its relation to other things. A symbol is a sign which arbitrarily or conventionally stands for its referent. A name is an identifier of a person, thing, or event (or of a class of persons, things, or events).

According to Sebeok, every sign has a referent (an object or thing to which it refers) or a referential domain (a class of objects or things to which it refers).

The Theory of Codes

Winfried Nöth (1990) explains that the meaning of the term "code" is ambiguous and that a semiotic code may be either a correlational device or an autonomous semiotic system. A cryptographic code is an example of a correlational device that may be used for translating messages from a primary sign system into messages of a secondary sign system (or secret code). A social or institutional code, on the other hand, is an example of an autonomous semiotic system that generates a system of meanings having behavioral implications.

Luis J. Prieto (1966) classifies semiotic codes according to their structural level of articulation. Codes may have *first articulation only*, *second articulation only*, *double articulation*, or *no articulation*. Codes with *first articulation only* can be analyzed into smaller meaningful units or signs, but not into *figurae*[13] (i.e. sign-elements that have no independent meaning). Codes with *second articulation only*

---

13. This term was coined by Hjemlslev, in *Prolegomena to a Theory of Language*, 1943.

cannot be analyzed into smaller meaningful units or signs, and they can only be analyzed into *figurae*. Codes with *double articulation* can be analyzed into signs and *figurae*. Codes with *no articulation* cannot be analyzed into signs or into *figurae*.[14]

A street sign that is analyzable into smaller meaningful elements is an example of a code with *first articulation only*. A numerical cataloging system is an example of a code with *second articulation only*. A verbal language, in which morphemes are articulated as phonemes or graphemes, is an example of a code with *double articulation*. A traffic light is an example of a code with *no articulation*.

According to Eco, some codes may also have *mobile articulation*, i.e. they may have signs which can become *figurae* or *figurae* which can become signs. An example is a card game in which the suits, such as hearts or clubs, are *figurae* which are combined with meaningful signs such as "king" or "queen", which in turn are elements of larger signs such as "full house" or "royal flush." If hearts are of greater value than clubs in a card game, however, these *figurae* may become signs.[15]

Daniel Chandler (2002) divides codes into three main types: social, textual, and interpretative. Social codes include codes of verbal language (phonological, syntactical, lexical), bodily codes (regarding bodily contact, proximity, facial expression, gaze, gestures, etc.), commodity codes (regarding commodities and manufactured goods), and behavioral codes (regarding protocols, rituals, roles, etc.) Textual codes include scientific codes, aesthetic codes, genre codes, rhetorical codes, stylistic codes, and mass media codes (photographic, televisual, filmic, etc.). Interpretative codes include perceptual codes and ideological codes. Each of these kinds of codes may be broadcast or narrowcast, depending on the range of audience to which they are directed.[16]

Semiotic codes may also be analogical or digital. Analogical codes correlate signs or elements that vary across a continuum, but digital codes correlate elements that are distinct or discrete. Examples of analogical signs are facial expressions, vocal qualities, colors, tastes, and smells. Examples of digital signs are words and numbers.

Roland Barthes (1974) describes five kinds of literary textual codes: semic (semantic), hermeneutic, proairetic (related to the sequence of action in a narrative), symbolic, and cultural. The five codes are interwoven voices that unite the

---

14. Eco, *A Theory of Semiotics*, pp. 232-3.
15. *Ibid.*, p. 233.
16. Daniel Chandler, *Semiotics: The Basics* (Abingdon, Routledge, 2002), p. 149.

fragments (*lexias*) of a text into a polyphonic whole. Thus, a text may have multiple codings, meanings, and readings.

Randall Harrison (1974) divides nonverbal code systems into two main types: 1) performance codes and 2) artifactual codes. Performance codes govern the use of bodily movements, such as facial expressions and hand gestures, while artifactual codes govern the use of artifacts, such as clothing, cosmetics, jewelry, cigarettes, motor vehicles, and buildings. Two additional types of nonverbal codes are 1) spatio-temporal codes (which govern the context in which communication occurs) and 2) mediatory codes (which govern the choice of options within a particular medium, such as film, photography, musical recording etc).

Nonverbal Communication

Language may be verbal or nonverbal. Nonverbal language involves the use of nonverbal signs (signs that are neither spoken nor written). Nonverbal language or communication does not involve the use of words, while verbal language involves the use of words. (Of note, vocal behaviors such as grunting or laughing are regarded as nonverbal behavior). While linguistics examines verbal aspects of communication, paralinguistics examines nonverbal aspects of communication. Paralinguistics is the study of paralanguage, but it is more specifically defined as the study of nonverbal aspects of vocal behavior.

The study of nonverbal communication includes 1) *paralinguistics* or *vocalics*, which studies the way in which vocal qualities such as pitch, range, accent, tempo, resonance, control, and intensity contribute to communication), 2) *kinesics* (which studies the way in which bodily movements, gestures, postures, and facial expressions contribute to communication), 3) *proxemics* (which studies the way in which interpersonal spatial relationships contribute to communication), 4) *oculesics* (which studies the role of the eyes in communication), 5) *haptics* (which studies tactile communication), 6) *aromatics* (which studies olfactory communication), 7) *edetics* (which studies gustatory communication), 8) *chronemics* (which studies time relationships in communication), 8) *melodics* (which studies the use of melody), and 9) *tectonics* (which studies the way in which nonverbal elements are assembled and structured).[17]

Within the context of a particular social setting, nonverbal behavior may reaffirm, complement, contradict, or substitute for verbal behavior. A person's non-

---

17. Randall P. Harrison, *Beyond Words: An Introduction to Communication* (Englewood Cliffs: Prentice-Hall, 1974), p. 72.

verbal behavior may provide clues as to how to interpret his or her verbal behavior. Nonverbal and verbal behavior may be inseparable aspects of any social interaction.[18]

Symbol and Metaphor

Symbols and metaphors are similar in some respects. Symbols may be metaphorical (some symbols may be metaphors), and metaphors may be symbolic. Symbols and metaphors may be verbal or nonverbal. An example of a nonverbal (visual) metaphor is the juxtaposition of two dissimilar images (e.g. a crowd of people and a flock of sheep) in a photograph, with an implied comparison of them. Another example of a visual metaphor is the sequential presentation of two dissimlar images in a television commercial (e.g. a person running and a rocket flying), with an implied comparison of them.

However, a difference between symbols and metaphors is that metaphors suggest a resemblance or similarity between two apparently different things. Symbols, on the other hand, do not necessarily have to resemble the things they represent. Symbols may be chosen arbitrarily, or they may be chosen because they have a resemblance to their referents. Words are an example of arbitrary symbols (although the sound of onomatopoeic words may resemble the things they represent).

A metaphor may be defined as an implied comparison of two things which are different in nature but which have something in common.[19] An example is the phrase, "A mighty fortress is our God" (which is the title of a hymn written by Martin Luther). Other examples are "The Lord is my shepherd" (Psalm 23:1), "The eye is the lamp of the body" (Matt. 6:22), "His enemies I will clothe with shame" (Psalm 132:18), and "Beware of false prophets who come to you in sheep's clothing but inwardly are ravenous wolves" (Matthew 7:15).

According to I.A. Richards (1936), a metaphor has two components: a *tenor* and a *vehicle*. The tenor of a metaphor is the subject to which various qualities are attributed, and the vehicle is the subject whose qualities are being attributed. The dissimilarity between the tenor and vehicle creates the *tension* of the metaphor, and the similarity between the tenor and vehicle is the *ground* of the metaphor.

---

18. Mark L. Knapp and Judith A. Hall, *Nonverbal Communication in Human Interaction* (Fort Worth: Holt, Rinehart and Winston, 1992), pp. 17-19.
19. Edward P.J. Corbett, *Classical Rhetoric for the Modern Student* (Oxford: Oxford University Press, 1990). P. 444.

The more remote is the resemblance between the tenor and vehicle, the greater is the tension of the metaphor.

Whether an expression is to be interpreted literally or metaphorically may be determined by whether there is a distinguishable difference between the tenor and vehicle of the expression. If the tenor and vehicle are indistinguishable from each other, then the expression may provisionally be interpreted literally. If the tenor and vehicle are distinguishable from each other, then the expression may be metaphorical. An expression may be simultaneously literal and metaphorical, and a single expression may simultaneously support multiple metaphors.[20]

In semiotic terms, the vehicle of a metaphor is the signifier, and the tenor of the metaphor is the signified idea or concept.

Other rhetorical tropes (figures of speech) that are related to metaphor include *simile* (explicit comparison of two different things, e.g. "All flesh is as grass, and all its glory like the flower of grass," 1 Peter 1:24, or "the kingdom of heaven is like a grain of mustard seed," Matt. 13:31), *synecdoche* (substitution of a part for the whole; for example, "where your treasure is, there will your heart be also," Matt. 6:21; or "he will guard the feet of his faithful ones; but the wicked shall be cut off in darkness," 1 Samuel 2:9), and *metonymy* (substitution of one word for another to which it is related; for example, "thy rod and thy staff, they comfort me," Psalm 23:4, which substitutes the rod and the staff for the person to whom they belong, the Lord).

George Lakoff and Mark Johnson (1980) describe several types of metaphors, including 1) *structural metaphors*, which enable us to structure concepts in terms of other concepts (e.g., the metaphor, "time is money"), 2) *organizational metaphors*, which enable us to assign concepts a spatial or temporal configuration (e.g., the metaphor,"I'm on top of the situation"), and 3) *ontological metaphors*, which allow us to refer to concepts as if they were beings or objects (e.g., the metaphor, "inflation has attacked the foundations of our economy").[21]

Lakoff and Johnson explain that metonymy may include the substitution of 1) the part for the whole (e.g., "The Giants need a stronger arm in right field"), 2) the producer for the product (e.g., "He bought a Ford"), 3) the object used for the user (e.g., "The gun he hired wanted fifty grand"), 4) the controller for the controlled (e.g. "Napoleon was defeated at Waterloo"), 5) the institution for the people responsible (e.g., "You'll never get the university to agree to that"), 6) the

---

20. I.A. Richards, *The Philosophy of Rhetoric* (New York: Oxford University Press, 1965), p. 119.
21. George Lakoff and Mark Johnson, *Metaphors We Live By* (Chicago: The University of Chicago Press, 1980), pp. 38-39.

place for the institution (e.g., "The White House isn't saying anything"), and 7) the place for the event (e.g., "Remember the Alamo").[22]

According to Lakoff and Johnson, most concepts that arise from everyday experience (e.g. concepts of time and place, concepts of causation, concepts of purpose, concepts of stages and of linear sequences, etc) are structured metaphorically. The understanding of concepts is, for the most part, metaphorically-emergent from experience rather than directly-emergent (although this distinction may be difficult to make in some cases, and some concepts may be both directly-emergent and structured metaphorically). Metaphors enable a given concept or conceptual domain to be understood in terms of other concepts or conceptual domains. Conceptual domains may be grounded on sensory experience, on reasoning and emotions, on changes in the physical environment, and on social interaction.

Lakoff and Johnson (1999) also describe metaphor as a cross-domain conceptual mapping. Primary metaphors map concepts from a source domain onto concepts in a target domain. Primary (atomic) metaphors may be combined to form complex (molecular) metaphors. Multiple metaphors may refer to a single concept (multiple concepts from a source domain may be mapped onto a single concept in a target domain). The aptness of a metaphor may be determined by whether it plays a significant role in structuring subjective experience, and by whether it has nonmetaphorical implications.

In the model proposed by Lakoff and Johnson, a single complex metaphorical mapping may have numerous submappings, e.g. in a single complex metaphor 1) the state of something may be conceptualized as a location, 2) a change in something may be conceptualized as a movement, 3) the cause of something may be conceptualized as a force, 4) the purpose of something may be conceptualized as a destination, 5) the means to something may be conceptualized as a path to a destination, 6) a difficulty may be conceptualized as an impediment to motion, 7) a freedom of action may be conceptualized as a lack of impediment to motion, 8) an event may be conceptualized as a moving object, or 9) a purposeful activity may be conceptualized as a journey. An event-structure metaphor may be a combination of multiple primary metaphors.[23]

Lakoff and Johnson explain that metaphorical mapping may have a figure-ground orientation. For example, in the time-as-movement metaphor, time may

---

22. *Ibid.*, pp. 38-39.
23. George Lakoff and Mark Johnson, *Philosophy in the Flesh: The Embodied Mind and its Challenge to Western Thought* (New York: Basic Books, 1999), p.179.

be conceptualized as a stream or figure moving past an observer who is the ground, or the observer may be conceptualized as a figure who is moving past a series of points in time which are the ground. Time metaphors may in some cases be figure-ground reversals of each other. The source domain of a metaphorical mapping that involves event-structure concepts cannot be completely neutral with respect to figure and ground.

Lakoff and Turner (1989) also explain that in every metaphorical mapping, slots in a source domain are mapped onto slots in a target domain, relations in a source domain are mapped onto relations in a target domain, properties in a source domain are mapped onto properties in a target domain, and knowledge in a source domain is mapped onto knowledge in a target domain. However, not all metaphors map conceptual structures onto other conceptual structures; e.g., an image metaphor may superimpose an image from a source domain onto an image in a target domain.[24]

Verbal Icons and Iconicity

W.K. Wimsatt, Jr. (1954) uses the term "verbal icon" for a visual image (especially a religious symbol), and he says that the verbal image that most fully realizes its verbal capacities is also an interpretation of reality in its metaphoric and symbolic dimensions.[25] However, this definition is somewhat confusing. A visual image may be evoked by a verbal image, but a visual image is a nonverbal image. Verbal images are not the same as nonverbal images. If a verbal icon is an image that most fully realizes its verbal capacities, what are those capacities? Moreover, the statement that a verbal icon is an interpretation of reality in its metaphoric and symbolic dimensions is ambiguous, because it does not answer the question of whether a verbal icon's interpretation of reality includes the metaphoric and symbolic dimensions of reality (this seems to be implied) or whether the verbal icon itself has metaphoric and symbolic dimensions (this is implied, but not explicitly stated). The classical semiotic definitions of iconicity by Peirce and Morris or the reinterpretation of iconicity by Eco appear to be more precise explanations of verbal iconicity.

---

24. George Lakoff and Mark Turner, *More than Cool Reason: A Field Guide to Poetic Metaphor* (Chicago: The University of Chicago Press, 1989), p. 89.
25. W.K. Wimsatt, Jr., *The Verbal Icon: Studies in the Meaning of Poetry* (University of Kentucky: University of Kentucky Press, 1954), p. x.

The Meaning of Signs

The "meaning" of a sign or symbol may be defined in many ways. C.K. Ogden and I.A. Richards (925) explain that in the case of symbols, the term "meaning" may refer to 1) the object to which the producer of a symbol actually refers, 2) the object to which the producer of a symbol ought to be referring, 3) the object to which the producer of a symbol intends to refer, 4) the object to which the interpreter of a symbol is actually referring, 5) the object to which the interpreter of a symbol believes himself to be referring, and 6) the object to which the interpreter of a symbol believes the producer to be referring. Ogden and Richards provide a list of seventeen other possible meanings of the term "meaning," and they conclude that it may be more useful to substitute terms such as "intention," "value," or "referent" for the processes involved in symbol situations.

Carl Wellman (1961) describes five kinds of meaning: descriptive, emotive, evaluative, directive, and critical. Descriptive statements tell us something about an event or situation. Emotive statements express an emotion that the speaker feels or could feel. Evaluative statements express a point of view toward something. Directive statements tell someone to do something. Critical statements modify, challenge, reject, or reaffirm the rationality of something. Statements may have more than one kind of meaning.

John Lyons (1995) explains that theories of meaning include 1) the referential or denotational theory (that the meaning of an expression is what it refers to or denotes), 2) the ideational or mentalistic theory (that the meaning of an expression is its ideational or conceptual representation in the mind of anyone who understands the expression), 3) the behaviorist theory (that the meaning of an expression is either the stimulus that evokes it or the response that it evokes, or a combination of both), 4) the meaning-is-use theory (that the meaning of an expression is determined by the way in which it is used as an instrument of language), 5) the verificationist theory (that the meaning of an expression is determined by the verifiability of the sentences or propositions containing it), and 6) the truth-conditional theory (that the meaning of an expression is its contribution to the truth-conditions of the phrases or sentences in which it is contained).[26]

Lyons distinguishes between word meaning (lexical meaning), sentence meaning, and utterance meaning. Word meaning is the meaning of words as units,

---

26. John Lyons, *Linguistic Semantics: An Introduction* (Cambridge: Cambridge University Press, 1995), p. 40.

while sentence meaning is determined not only by the meaning of words as units, but also by their grammatical structure. Sentence meaning differes from utterance meaning in being highly independent of context. Utterance meaning depends, at least to some degree, on context, and it also depends on the use or purpose of an utterance as a speech act.

Chapter III

THEMATIC PARADIGMS

The Sacramental Sign

The question of whether the bread and wine of the holy eucharist are merely symbols of Christ's body and blood or whether they are literally changed into Christ's body and blood has, for centuries, generated controversy among the various denominations of the Church. There has also been controversy about how the term "sacrament" should be defined.

Saint Augustine (354-430 C.E.) defines a sacrament as a visible sign of an invisible grace. It is a sacred sign of a divine reality, which conveys that reality to us. Thus, according to his definition, such things as prayers and blessings are sacraments, if they are efficacious in bestowing grace on us.

Hugh of St. Victor (c.1078-1141) defines a sacrament as a physical or material element that both signifies and contains by its own sanctification an invisible and spiritual grace. Not all signs of sacred things are sacraments. In order to be defined as a sacrament, a sign must 1) bear a likeness to the thing of which it is the sacrament, 2) be instituted in such a way that it is ordained to signify that thing, 3) have been sanctified in such a way that it contains that thing, and 4) be efficacious in conferring that thing on those who are sanctified. Thus, Hugh of St. Victor does not consider penance to be a sacrament, since it has no physical or material sign.[1]

Peter Lombard (c.1100-1164) says that a sacrament resembles the sacred thing of which it is a sign and that its purpose is not only to signify that sacred thing but to sanctify the believer. Signs whose purpose is only to signify things are not sacraments. Signs which do not resemble the things that they signify are also not sacraments. Lombard says that the sacraments include baptism, confirmation, the eucharist, penance, marriage, ordination, and extreme unction.

Saint Thomas Aquinas (1225-1274) approaches the question of the real presence of Christ in the eucharistic bread and wine by making a distinction between substance and accident. He says that sacraments are signs of commemoration of Christ's sufferings for us, of the grace that those sufferings bestow on us, and of the eternal life that we may thereby attain. The eucharist is a sacramental sign by which the substance of bread and wine are transformed into the substance of Christ's body and blood. This is a process of "transubstantiation." The accidental features of the bread and wine (their physical reality) remain as a sign of the spiritual reality which they have attained. In this connection, an accident is some-

---

1. "Hugh of St. Victor on the Definition of a Sacrament," in *The Christian Theology Reader*, edited by Alister E. McGrath (Oxford: Blackwell, 1995), p. 531.

thing whose essence is to have existence in something other than itself, while a substance is something whose essence is to have existence *not* in something other than itself.

Thus, the doctrine of "real presence" affirms that there is a real presence and not merely a symbolic presence of Christ in the bread and wine of the holy eucharist. However, this doctrine has not been universally accepted by all Christians. Roman Catholics have accepted it, while Baptists and Evangelicals have rejected it. Other denominations of the Church have said merely that the presence of Christ in the eucharist is a mystery.

An important question to be considered is whether the real presence of Christ in the eucharistic bread and wine is also an actual presence. To say that the eucharist "really" contains the body and blood of Christ may imply that the eucharist actually contains Christ's body and blood, but the relation between reality and actuality is left unexplained. If the real presence is both real and actual, then the term "real presence" leaves this unstated, and the question remains as to which modality of being comes into play when the sacrament is administered. Is the presence of Christ in the bread and wine actualized as well as realized in the eucharist? If the term "real presence" implies that real presence is more than actual presence, how important is it for this real presence to be actualized?

Reality does not necessarily imply actuality. The real may be possible, actual, or necessary. The real-possible may be just as real as the real-actual or the real-necessary. Furthermore, actuality does not necessarily imply reality The ideal may be just as actual as the real, and ideal actuality does not necessarily imply real actuality.

There is also the question of whether the bread and wine are merely signs of Christ's presence or whether they themselves are the reality of Christ's presence. If they are the reality of Christ's presence, then the question arises as to whether they are any different from people or things that convey Christ's presence elsewhere in the world.

Martin Luther (1483-1546) says that there is a real presence of Christ in the eucharist, but he rejects the doctrine of transsubstantiation. He says that there are three, and not seven, sacraments: baptism, penance, and holy communion. The substance of the body of Christ is present in the eucharist, along with the substance of the bread and wine. In order for divinity to dwell within a physical body, it is not necessary for the substance of that body to be transsubstantiated. Both divine substance and physical substance may be present in the same physical body. Thus, "consubstantiation" occurs in the eucharist.

John Calvin (1509-1564) defines a sacrament as an outward sign by which God reassures us of his good will and supports us despite the weakness of our faith. It is also a sign that enables us to demonstrate our piety toward God. God makes allowance for our earthly nature by giving us a visible sign of his grace.

Theodore Beza (1519-1605), a French Protestant theologian who was a friend of John Calvin, defines a sacrament as an external sign of a divine and heavenly reality. In order to be defined as a sacrament, a sign must be efficacious in conveying divine grace. Holy communion does not change the physical substance of the bread and wine. There is instead a change in the purpose for which they are used. They are used no longer for physical sustenance alone, but for the purpose of revealing the mystery of salvation.

Huldrych (Ulrich) Zwingli (1484-1531), a leader of the Protestant Reformation in Switzerland, takes a more radical view by denying the real presence of Christ in the eucharist. According to Zwingli, a sacrament is a sign of a sacred thing. A sign cannot be the same as the thing that it signifies. If it were, then it would be the thing itself and would not be a sign. A sign and the thing it signifies cannot be one and the same. Therefore, the eucharistic bread is not the same as the body of Christ. This is why Jesus, after saying, "This is my body, which is given for you," then said "do this in remembrance of me" (Luke 22:19). He was not saying "This is literally my body"; he was saying, "This signifies my body." He was speaking figuratively, in the same way that he was speaking figuratively when he said, "I am the true vine, and my Father is the vinedresser. Every branch of mine that bears no fruit, he takes away, and every branch that does not bear fruit he prunes, that it may bear more fruit" (John 15:1-2). The eucharist is a commemoration of the fact that Christ atoned for our sins by his suffering and death. The bread and wine are reminders of his body and blood. They are tokens in commemoration of his sacrifice for us.

Zwingli also says that a sacrament is a sign that we repent of our sins and that we wish to make amends for our past transgressions. By receiving the sacrament, we pledge ourselves to follow the example of Jesus' life. The eucharist signifies that in thankfulness we will embrace our brethren with the same love that Christ showed when he redeemed and saved us.[2]

Holy baptism is an external sign of an internal faith, redemption, and salvation, says Zwingli. It is a pledge that we dedicate ourselves to Father, Son, and Holy Ghost. It reminds us that John the Baptist said, "I baptize you with water

---

2. Ulrich Zwingli, "An Exposition of the Faith," in *Zwingli and Bullinger*, edited and translated by G.W. Bromiley (Philadelphia: The Westminster Press, 1953), p. 249.

for repentance, but he who is coming after me is mightier than I, whose sandals I am not worthy to carry; he will baptize you with the Holy Spirit and with fire" (Matt. 4:11). Thus, baptism with water is an external baptism, but baptism with fire is an internal, spiritual baptism. Immersion in water signifies burial in Christ, just as Christ died and was buried. Reemergence from water signifies the resurrection of Christ.[3] Baptism also signifies that Christ has washed us of our sins and that we are to lead new lives in his name.

Edward Schillebeeckx (1968) takes a position that is compatible with the doctrine of transsubstantiation, by saying that the change which the eucharistic bread and wine undergo is actually not a change in their physical reality, but a change in their function and signification. Thus, transsubstantiation is actually a transfunctionalization or transsignification. The bread and wine signify not a gift from Christ, who gives himself in them, but Christ himself as "living, personal presence." They are a sign that makes Christ's presence real to us, but they are also a sign that brings about the real presence of the Church. Thus, there is reciprocity in the "real presence."[4]

The Dynamics of Presence and Absence

The presence-absence paradigm is a key to understanding Christian semiotics. Since a sign is something that stands for something else, a sign may also be a substitute for something that is not immediately accessible to sensory experience. Indeed, the purpose of a sign may be to act as a substitute for something that is not immediately accessible to sensory experience. If the object of the sign were immediately accessible to sensory experience, then the sign would be unnecessary.

Thus, there may be a question of whether the production of signs and symbols to signify God is an attempt to restore the presence of God in the face of a perceived absence. The dialectic of presence and absence may also be the dialectic of faith and doubt. Symbols of religious faith may reassure us of God's presence in the world.

According to Jacques Derrida (1974), absence may present itself as absence within the presence of a trace. A trace is an indication (signifier) of a presence within an absence, but it is also an indication of an absence within a presence. A trace may itself bear traces of other signifiers. Thus the meaning of a signifier can never be reduced to merely presence or absence, and it is defined by the play of

---

3. *Ibid.*, p. 151.
4. Edward Schillebeeckx, *The Eucharist* (New York: Burns & Oates, 1968), p. 139.

difference between them. The "metaphysics of presence" attempts to freeze the play of difference between presence and absence, but it loses their dynamic and changing meaning by privileging presence over absence. The metaphysical opposition of presence and absence is also the opposition of the signifier and the signified, and thus the metaphysics of presence attempts to construct a transcendental signified, i.e. a signified that transcends all signifiers.

If, as Derrida suggests, there can be no transcendental signified, then either God must be someone (or something) who cannot be signified and who transcends signification or the transcendental signified must be only another signifier of God.

On the other hand, Jesus as symbol of God is both the signifier and the signified. As symbol of God and as redeemer, he is the signifier that signifies itself. He is also a perfect symbol, a signifier with an unlimited capacity for meaning and signification. God signifies himself through Christ.

Jean Baudrillard (1994) takes a different approach by describing the presence-absence paradigm in terms of the opposition between dissimulation and simulation. Dissimulation implies the presence of something that the dissimulator attempts to conceal, but simulation implies the absence of something that the simulator attempts to replace with a surrogate. Dissimulation leaves the principle of reality intact, but simulation threatens the difference between truth and falsehood, between the real and the imaginary.[5] Simulacra tend to multiply until there is no reality and there is only a hyperreality. If God can be simulated or reduced to the signs of faith, then faith becomes nothing but a simulacrum. Thus, there is a difference between using symbols as signifiers of God and using symbols as simulations of God.

The Conflict between Religious Iconism and Iconoclasm

Reverence for religious symbols may sometimes degenerate into idolatory and iconolatry. Exodus 20:2-5 says, "And God spoke all these words, saying, 'I am the Lord your God, who brought you out of the land of Egypt, out of the house of bondage. You shall have no other gods before me. You shall not make for yourself a graven image, or any likeness of anything that is in heaven above, or that is in the earth beneath, or that is in the water under the earth; you shall not bow down

---

5. Jean Baudrillard, *Simulacra and Simulation*, translated by Sheila Faria Glaser (Ann Arbor: The University of Michigan Press, 1994), p. 3.

to them or serve them.'" Deuteronomy 4:16 also says, "beware lest you act corruptly by making a graven image for yourselves." Isaiah 31:7 says, "For in that day, everyone shall cast away his idols of silver and his idols of gold, which your hands have sinfully made for you." And Isaiah 45:20 also says, "They have no knowledge who carry about their wooden idols and keep on praying to a god that cannot save."

Iconoclasm was a religious movement that began in the Byzantine empire in the eighth and ninth centuries C.E. and that rejected as idolatrous the veneration of religious icons (i.e. statues, paintings, and other symbolic images). According to the Iconoclastic Council (Ecumenical Synod) of Constantinople (754 C.E.), iconism debases the nature of worship by venerating created objects instead of God the Creator. To produce a physical image of Christ is to attempt to depict something divine that cannot be depicted, or it is to attempt to separate the physical from the divine nature of Christ and to represent the physical nature of Christ as something not divine. Thus, the only acceptable icon is the bread and wine of the Eucharist, since it becomes the actual body and blood of Jesus Christ.

The Visible and the Invisible

The nature of the interplay between presence and absence is indicated by Paul's Letter to the Philippians (2:12): "Therefore my beloved, as you have always obeyed, so now, not only as in my presence but much more in my absence, work out your own salvation with fear and trembling; for God is at work in you." Paul also says in 1 Cor. 5:3, "For though absent in body, I am present in spirit, and as if present, I have already pronounced judgment in the name of the Lord Jesus."

Other thematic paradigms (binary oppositions) that have an important role in Christian semiotics include visible-invisible, darkness-light, body-spirit, sin-righteousness, and doubt-faith.

Paul says of Jesus in 1 Col. 15-16, "He is the image of the invisible God, the first-born of all creation; for in him all things were created, in heaven and on earth, visible and invisible." And in Romans 1:19-20, Paul says, "For what can be known about God is plain to them, because God has shown it to them. Ever since the creation of the world his invisible nature, namely, his eternal power and deity, has been clearly perceived in the things that have been made." Indeed, a fundamental aspect of Christian faith, i.e. faith in Christ's resurrection, may be a basis for the belief that Christ's resurrection was physical (or something that could be visibly confirmed by his physical appearance) as well as spiritual.

The Seen and the Unseen

The paradigm of visible-invisible is also that of seen-unseen. The Nicene Creed says, "We believe in one God, the Father, the Almighty, maker of heaven and earth, of all that is, seen and unseen." Hebrews 11:1 says, "Now faith is the assurance of things hoped for, the conviction of things not seen." 2 Cor. 4:17-18 says, "For this slight momentary affliction is preparing for us an eternal weight of glory beyond all comparison, because we look not to the things that are seen but to the things that are unseen; for the things that are seen are transient, but the things that are unseen are eternal."

Body and Spirit

The body-spirit paradigm is reflected by the teachings of the Gospels that the Church is the body of Christ. Each member of the Church is a part of Christ's body. God made Jesus "the head over all things for the Church, which is his body, the fullness of him who fills all in all" (Eph. 1:22-23). "For just as the body is one and has many members, and all the members of the body, though many, are one body, so it is with Christ. For by one Spirit we were all baptized into one body" (1 Cor. 12:12-13). The Gospels teach us that we may each have a different function as members of one body. "For as in one body we have many members, and all the members do not have the same function, so we, though many, are one body in Christ, and individually members one of another. Having gifts according to the grace given to us, let us use them; if prophesy, in proportion to our faith; if service, in our serving; he who teaches, in his teaching" (Rom. 12:4-7).

Thus, we may each have a different calling, and we may each have a different role to play in the life of the Church. We may each, in our own unique way, be able to contribute to the functioning of the Church as the body of Christ.

Saint Augustine says that Christ is both the head and body of the Church. Head and body are the Christ and the Church together (Sermon 341). However, the Second Vatican Council (1962-5) says that Christ is the head *of* the body which is the Church. This statement is based on what is said in the scriptures (Col. 1:18: "He is the head of the body, the Church," and Eph. 4:15-16, "we are to grow up in every way into him who is the head, into Christ, from whom the whole body, joined and knit together by every joint with which it is supplied, when each part is working properly, makes bodily growth and upbuilds itself in love").

What kind of body is the Church? Pope Pius XII, in his 1943 encyclical, *Mystici Corporis Christi* (*On the Mystical Body of Christ*), says that the Church is both a visible and mystical body. The Church is the mystical rather than physical body of Christ, because the physical body of Christ sits at the right hand of the Father. Christ is the head of the Church, and he is also the savior of his body.

In the Bible, the church is also described as a field of God (1 Cor. 3:9), as a vineyard (Matt. 21:33, Isaiah 5:1-2), as a flock of sheep, of whom the Lord is the shepherd (Isaiah 40:11; John 10:11), as a building of God (1 Cor. 3:9), as the bride of Christ (Eph. 5:23), and as the New Jerusalem (Rev. 21:2).

Sin and Righteousness

The sin-righteousness paradigm is presented by Romans 6:12-14: "Let not sin therefore reign in your mortal bodies, to make you obey their passions. Do not yield your members to sin as instruments of wickedness, but yield yourself to God as men who have been brought from death to life, and your members to God as instruments of righteousness. For sin will have no dominion over you, since you are not under law but under grace." Other references to this paradigm include Romans 3:9 and 2 Corinthians 5:21.

Faith and Doubt

The opposition of faith and doubt is described by Matthew 14:31, "Jesus immediately reached out his hand and caught him, saying to him, 'O man of little faith, why did you doubt?'" James 1:6 also says, "But let him ask in faith, with no doubting, for he who doubts is like a wave of the sea that is driven and tossed by the wind."

Paul Tillich (1957) explains that every act of faith recognizes that there is a possibility for doubt. The dynamics of faith require the recognition that faith does not exclude uncertainty. Non-dynamic (conventional) faith may suppress doubt, but faith as an act of ultimate concern requires an individual to have the courage to make a personal commitment and to recognize the possibility of uncertainty.

Saint Augustine, in his *Enchiridion* (421-2), says that faith, hope, and love are mutually dependent. Without love, faith has nothing through which to act, and without faith, hope cannot exist. Faith is a gift from God, and it cannot be attained through good works alone. At the same time, faith is expressed through good works. Faith includes 1) faith in God the Creator, 2) faith in Christ the

Redeemer, 3) faith in the forgiveness of sins, and 4) faith in the resurrection of the body, and in everlasting life.

Signs and Non-Signs

Saint Augustine, in *De Doctrina Christiana* (*On Christian Doctrine*, 397-426) says that signs are things that are used to signify other things. Signs may be "natural" or "conventional." Natural signs (e.g. smoke as a sign of fire) are not intended to signify anything, but conventional signs are intended to signify something. All signs are "things," but not all things are signs. Thus, the world may consist of signs and non-signs.

However, it may be argued that all things are signs of divine will. If all things depend for their being on God's will, then their being must in some way be a "sign" of God's will.

Every sign must be a sign *of* something. A sign can only be a sign by referring to (signifying or standing for) something. As Saussure explained, a sign depends for its existence on both a signifier and a signified.

A signifier must therefore have an object to which it refers (a referent). However, not all signifers (i.e. sign-vehicles) refer to things that actually exist. The truth or falsehood of signs may depend on whether they signify things that actually exist. In every sign, however, there must be something signified by the signifier, and the signifier therefore presupposes the signified.

Any sign of God therefore presupposes (the existence of) God. Signs of God may be revelations, and revelations may be signs of God. God's presence is revealed, directly and indirectly, to us through signs that strengthen our faith.

To the extent that God acts through us, we may all signify, through our actions, God's love for humankind. Our actions may signify our faith (or lack of faith) in God and our obedience (or disobedience) to the Word of God.

To the extent that we think, act, and communicate symbolically and are therefore engaged in the study of signs and symbols, we are all semioticians or practitioners of semiotics. When we study the life of Jesus and his teachings, we are studying signs of God.

The signs through which God is revealed are sacred. They are sanctified by acting as vehicles of God's grace, love and truth. Thus, sanctification may be a sign-process by which a sign conveys God's grace and is imbued with the Holy Spirit.

The Power of Sacred Signs

Stigmata (marks or wounds on a person's body that resemble the wounds on the crucified body of Jesus) are an example of signs that may be regarded as holy or sacred (and therefore as blasphemous if they are self-inflicted by an impostor). Stigmata may be regarded as emblems of sanctity (for example, Saint Francis of Assisi is said to have developed stigmata on his body while he was praying).

Holy water is a symbol of spiritual purification and of God's blessing. It is used to administer the sacrament of Holy Baptism, to anoint the sick, and to adminster other rites of blessing.

Holy relics, such as the shroud of Turin (about whose authenticity there is controversy), and mysterious phenomena such as weeping statues of the Virgin Mary and bleeding statues of Jesus have shown that religious icons can hold an extraordinary fascination for those who view them as signs from God. The Holy Grail as a symbol of the quest for spiritual redemption has, for centuries, been a subject of literature, drama, and art.

What is the source of the power of such symbols? What is the source of the power of Jesus' message?

The power of Jesus' message may be partly due to the fact that he spoke from a position of not only moral but divine authority. Through his life and his teachings, he revealed his oneness with God. When he delivered his Sermon on the Mount, the crowd was astonished at his teachings, because he taught them "as one who had authority, and not as their scribes" (Matthew 7:29). After the Last Supper, as he spoke to his disciples, Philip asked him to show them the Father, and Jesus said, "Do you not believe that I am in the Father and the Father in me? The words that I speak to you I do not speak on my own authority; but the Father who dwells in me does his works. Believe me that I am in the Father and the Father in me; or else believe me for the sake of the works themselves" (John: 14:10-11).

When the high priest asks Jesus, "Are you the Christ, the Son of the Blessed?" Jesus says, "I am; and you will see the Son of man sitting at the right hand of power, and coming with the clouds of heaven" (Mark 14:61-62).

The power of Jesus' message did not come from his words and actions alone, but from the source of those words and actions, God. The life of Jesus was a unity of Word and Act. His words and actions were in unity with the Word of God. He gave his life in sacrifice so that we could be redeemed from our sins and so that his obedience could become ours, by faith.

According to the Second Vatican Council (1962-5), the obedience of faith (Romans 1:5) consists of giving ourselves to God, of freely committing our whole selves to God, and of freely assenting to the truth revealed by God. Obedience is possible through divine grace. God can open our minds and hearts to the truth of his Word by revealing himself to us.

Matthew 12:38-40 says that Jesus was asked by some of the scribes and Pharisees to give a sign but that he refused and said, "An evil and adulterous generation seeks for a sign; but no sign shall be given to it except the sign of the prophet Jonah." Jesus also said, "For as Jonah became a sign to the men of Nineveh, so will the Son of man be to this generation" (Luke 11:30).

While the atheist may say that there is no such thing as a sign from God, the skeptic may suspend judgment, and the agnostic may say that it is impossible to know with complete certainty whether any given thing is a sign from God.

Signs may be intentional or unintentional. Intentionality may or may not be attributed to a sign by an interpreter (i.e. the interpreter may or may not assume that the producer of a sign intentionally produced it). Presumably, intentionality belongs to all signs of God, since a sign of God could not occur unless it were in accordance with God's will.

The Parables of Jesus

Jesus delivered many of his teachings in the form of parables. Thus, he spoke a symbolic language. His parables required decoding by their interpreters. (The use of a code to produce signs and symbols establishes a correlation between the expression of signs and their content, so that producers and interpreters of signs can share the same understanding of their meaning.). The reason why his teachings were delivered in the form of coded messages is problematic. Why didn't he speak in a language that could be understood by everyone? According to Matthew 13:34-35, everything that Jesus said was in the form of parables: "All this, Jesus said to the crowds in parables; indeed he said nothing to them without a parable. This was to fulfill what was spoken by the prophet: 'I will open my mouth in parables, I will utter what has been hidden since the foundation of the world.'"

Among the many parables of Jesus are the parable of the sower (Matt. 13:3-23, Mark 4:2-20, Luke 8:4-15), the parable of new wine in old skins (Matt. 9:17, Mark 2:22, Luke 5:37-38), the parable of the two sons (Matt. 21:28-32), the parable of the good Samaritan (Luke 10:30-37), the parable of the mustard seed (Matt. 13:31-32, Mark 4:30-32), the parable of the lost son (Luke 15:11-

32), the parable of the Pharisee and the tax collector (Luke 15:11-32), and the parable of the lillies of the field (Matt. 6:25-33, Luke 12:22-31).

The explanation for Jesus' use of parables is provided by the following verses: "Then the disciples came and said to him, 'Why do you speak in parables?' And he answered them, 'To you it has been given to know the secrets of the kingdom of heaven, but to them it has not been given ... This is why I speak to them in parables, because seeing they do not see, and hearing they do not hear, nor do they understand'" (Matthew 13:10-13). Thus, in order to understand the meaning of Jesus' parables, we must first have accepted God's will. We cannot understand with our minds unless we have already understood with our hearts. If we have not truly committed ourselves to God, then seeing, we will not see, and hearing, we will not hear. The parables can only be understood by those who, in their hearts, have truly accepted God.

In order to interpret the meaning of Jesus' parables, we must be aware of our own preconceptions regarding what he is saying or instructing us to do, and we must recognize that our preconceptions may sometimes hinder our understanding or lead to our misunderstanding. H.-G. Gadamer (1975) explains that the meaning of a text or of a particular mode of discourse may always be further interpreted. To try to reduce the meaning of a text to whatever is discoverable at a particular point in time is to try to deprive the text of its full meaning. The interpretation of a text does not require us to abandon all of our preconceptions of its meaning, but it requires us to be aware of our preconceptions and to be aware of how they may contribute to our understanding or to our misunderstanding of the text. The hermeneutic experience also requires us to recognize that the nature of our understanding may change over a period of time, and that our understanding of the meaning of a text is always influenced by our own historical situation.

The Word of God as Message and Revelation

God speaks to us through Jesus, through the prophets, through saints, and through everyday experiences in our lives. There is a sense in which God speaks through us when we act according to the will of God. Our actions may be a kind of language through which divine grace, divine love, and divine truth are capable of being communicated.

There may also be a "message" that is transmitted by those who speak the Word of God. Insofar as it is a "message," it may have an informational content. It may be coded and transmitted as a stream of data. It may be addressed by a sender (God) to a receiver (humankind). It may be capable of being transmitted or broadcast over various media.

According to Roman Jakobson (1960), the constitutive factors of any act of verbal communication include 1) an addresser (the sender or encoder of a message), 2) a message, 3) a context (referent), 4) a contact (a physical channel and a psychological connection between the addresser and the addressee), 5) a code which is at least partially shared by the addresser and the addressee, and 6) an addressee. In order for verbal communication to occur, the message must also be capable of being verbalized by the addresser, and the addressee must be capable of receiving and decoding the message. Each constitutive factor of communication determines a different function of language. The *emotive* (or expressive) function of language is oriented toward the addresser. The *poetic* function of language focuses on the message for its own sake. The *referential* function of language is oriented toward the context. The *phatic* (i.e. pertaining to social purpose more than informational content) function of language serves to establish, maintain, or discontinue communication and thus is oriented to the contact. The *metalingual* function of language ensures that the addresser and addressee are using the same code. And the *conative* (i.e. pertaining to striving or to causing action) function of language is oriented toward the addressee. Verbal messages may fulfill more than one of these six functions, but their structure may be determined by which function predominates in any given act of commmunication.[6]

Communication may occur by means of transmission of signs and signals. Signals may not signify anything and therefore may not necessarily be signs (a signal that signifies something is a sign). A signalling system may include a sender, a signal, a channel through which the signal is sent, and a receiver. The sender may utilize a transmitter to send the signal to the receiver. The information that is conveyed by the signal may be encoded by the sender and decoded by the receiver. Coding of the sign or signal may provide methods of error detection and may increase the accuracy and efficiency of transmission. The signalling system may also require a method of reducing interference from outside "noise" along the channel, so that the integrity of the signal can be maintained during transmission.

Theoretically, a divine message to humankind may have an unlimited informational capacity. However, the human intellect may only be capable of processing a finite amount of information at any given time. The question therefore

---

6. Roman Jakobson, "Closing Statement: Linguistics and Poetics," in *Style in Language*, edited by Thomas A. Sebeok (Cambridge: The M.I.T. Press, 1960), pp. 353-7.

arises as to whether God's message must be delivered in finite units or segments if we are to be capable of understanding it. The question also arises as to whether God's message is always delivered in such a way that it is capable of being understood by those who have faith. If it can be delivered in an infinite number of ways, then God's grace must be necessary in order for us to understand it.

There may be messengers to whom God has spoken, whom God has chosen to deliver his Word. There may also be those who (truly or falsely) believe that they have heard a divine message and who (truly or falsely) believe that they have been chosen to be messengers.

However, Paul Tillich (1951) says that although the Word is a medium of revelation, it is not simply information. It is a transformational power. According to Tillich, the Word is 1) a principle of divine self-manifestation, 2) a medium of creation, 3) the manifestation of the divine life in the history of revelation, 4) the manifestation of the divine life in the final revelation, 5) the document of the final revelation, and 6) the message of the Church as proclaimed in its preaching and teaching.[7]

The Word of God may be revealed by scripture, by divine revelation, and by faith. Insofar as it may be delivered in the form of a lesson or teaching, it may be capable of being learned or taught. Those who speak the Word of God may be both messengers and teachers.

According to Karl Barth (1936), the Word of God has a threefold form, in that it may be understood as revelation, as scripture, and as proclamation. Scripture and proclamation may be based on revelation, but these three forms of the Word do not differ in value. The Word of God is a threefold unity which is identical to God, Jesus Christ, and the Holy Spirit. It is also the "speech" of God, and as an act of speech it can be heard and understood by those who have faith in it.

Divine revelation may be an event in which (or a process by which) the Word of God is spoken to us and we recognize its authenticity, authority, relevance, and meaning. Revelation may itself be revealed by obedience to the Word. Revelation may also be a process by which we recognize signs of God's presence and correctly interpret their signification. Signs of God are "theophanies" (appearances of God) which, through God's grace, may be recognized, understood, and communicated to others through our moral conduct.

---

7. Paul Tillich, *Systematic Theology, Volume I* (Chicago, The University of Chicago Press, 1951), pp. 157-9.

The Truth of Signs

Signs may be interpreted correctly or incorrectly. Causes of incorrect interpretation of signs may include misperceptions, misleading preconceptions, hasty generalizations, vagueness or ambiguity of signs, and resemblances between true and false signs. Errors in the interpretation of linguistic or non-linguistic signs may also be caused by delusions, hallucinations, or other cognitive disorders.

Morris (1971) says that the adequacy of a sign may be determined by whether it produces a disposition in the interpreter to initiate the response that would occur if the object or event which is denoted by the sign were the actual stimulus. Thus, the truth of signs is not the same as their adequacy, since true signs may in some cases be inadequate to produce a disposition in the interpreter to initiate a particular response, and false signs may in some cases be adequate.to produce a disposition in the interpreter to initiate a particular response.

Tillich (1951) says that the truth of a religious symbol is different from the truth of other symbols, because it is not necessarily related to the truth of the empirical assertions involved in it. A religious symbol "has truth" if it is adequate to the revelation it expresses, and it "is true" if it expresses a true revelation. Thus, the truth of religious symbols may have a double meaning.[8]

We must keep in mind, however, that not all symbols are propositional or capable of being judged as true or false. Various epistemological problems may also occur if we do not make a distinction between subjective truth and objective truth.

Anthropomorphism and Gender Symbolism

Many symbolic expressions for attributes of God may be susceptible to the criticism that they reinforce anthropomorphic conceptions of God. For example, such expressions as "the hand of God" (Acts 7:55-60), "the mouth of God" (Matthew 4:4), and "the face of God" (Genesis 32:30) suggest that God has a human form or is similar to a human being. The Nicene Creed says, "On the third day he rose again in accordance with the Scriptures, he ascended into heaven and is seated at the right hand of the Father." The Acts of the Apostles (7:56) says, Stephen "gazed into the heaven and saw the glory of God, and Jesus standing at the right hand of God; and he said, 'Behold, I see the heavens opened, and the Son of man standing at the right hand of God.'" In Genesis 32:30, Jacob says,

---

8. *Ibid.*, p. 240.

"For I have seen God face to face, and yet my life is preserved." The face-to-face metaphor suggests that we can have a dialogue with God, but it also suggests that we can be on the same ontological level as, or somehow coequal to, God.

Mary Daly (1973) explains that the gender symbolism of calling God "Father" and of thereby assigning to God a male gender tends to perpetuate gender stereotypes, and that it thus tends to contribute to the social oppression of women. We need to develop a new language with which to talk about God, says Daly. Our theological language must be more inclusive and must transcend gender differences. The notion that anthropomorphic symbols for God are necessary in order to make the universe seem less impersonal is a misconception. There need be no dichotomy between human beings and cosmic power.[9]

Rebecca Chopp (1989) describes the Word of God as the perfectly open sign, the sign that reveals the full inclusivity of discourse. The Word is the sign of all signs, the sign that is always open to new signification. Furthermore, the Word makes possible the symbolic capacity of language. It sustains and redeems all signs and symbols in their continuing signification.[10]

The Report of the Commission on Theology and Church Relations of the Lutheran Church-Missouri Synod (1998) recognizes the need for more inclusive and gender-neutral language in presentation of the scriptures, but it argues that the scriptures are not merely the rendering of a culturally-based interpretation of God. The scriptures are divine revelation, and the language of divine revelation transcends cultural circumstances. The Commission says that translation of the Bible must therefore be faithful to the actual text as it has been given to us. To change the language of the Bible to more gender-neutral language is to try to neutralize its meaning, and the gender imagery of the Bible must therefore be respected. At the same time, we should remember that God transcends gender categories and that revelation is given equally to all of us.[11]

Some other issues related to the question of whether a less gender-specific methodology can be used in translating the Bible are that any translation, to some extent, changes the meaning of language, and the meaning of language changes over a period of time. The meaning of language is influenced by its his-

---

9. Mary Daly, *Beyond God the Father: Toward a Philosophy of Women's Liberation* (Boston: Beacon Press, 1973), p. 33.
10. Rebecca S. Chopp, *The Power to Speak: Feminism, Language, God* (New York, Crossroad Publishing Company, 1989), pp. 30-32.
11. *Biblical Revelation and Inclusive Language: A Report of the Commission on Theology and Church Relations of the Lutheran Church-Missouri Synod, February 1998*. St Louis: The Luteran Church-Missouri Synod, 1996.

torical setting, and the same words that are used in one cultural context may have quite a different meaning in another cultural context.

Other Sacred Signs

The transfiguration of Jesus is a symbolic event in which his physical appearance is transformed so that it reflects his true glory. Jesus leads Peter, James, and John up a mountain, and his physical appearance suddenly changes, so that his face shines like the sun, and his garments become dazzling white. Elijah and Moses then appear, and a voice from an overshadowing cloud says, "This is my beloved Son, with whom I am well pleased; listen to him." As Jesus and the disciples are coming back down the mountain, he instructs them not to reveal what they have seen until he has been raised from the dead (Mark 9:2-13).

According to Martin Luther (1522), signs of the second coming of Christ will include humanity's failure to recognize that the day of judgment is at hand. Other signs will include humanity's preoccupation with sensual and worldly pleasures. Natural signs will include a dimming of the sun and a falling of the stars from the heavens. Other signs will include earthquakes, famine, pestilence, and wars.

The phenomenon of "speaking in tongues" (incomprehensible speech as an ecstatic form of worship inspired by the Holy Spirit) is an example of the human need to express religious feelings symbolically. The Acts of the Apostles (19:5-6) says, "On hearing this, they were baptized in the name of the Lord Jesus. And when Paul had laid his hands upon them, the Holy Spirit came upon them; and they spoke with tongues and prophesied."

Miracles are extraordinary and supernatural occurrences which may be interpreted to be signs of divine providence. Miracles that Jesus performed included changing water into wine (John 2:1-11), feeding 5000 people with 5 loaves of bread and 2 fish (Matthew 14:13-21), walking on water (Matthew 14:22-33), healing the lame and the blind (Matthew 15:30-31), and raising a dead man, Lazarus, to life (John 11:1-44). Miracles that Moses performed included changing water into blood (Exodus 7:14-24), turning a rod into a serpent (Exodus 7:8-13), drawing water from a rock (Exodus 17:5-5), and dividing the waters of the Red Sea (Exodus 14:21-22). Thus, miracles are also signs of God's power, which may be performed in order to convince those who are lacking in faith.

The Semiotics of Interpersonal Dialogue

The recognition that words, signs, and symbols may be more than a means of transmitting information and that they may also be a means of establishing a mutual relation between ourselves and God is a basic principle of Martin Buber's philosophy of dialogue. Buber's philosophy has been described as a dialogic personalism, because it views the relation between ourselves and God as an interpersonal relation in which we can engage in dialogue with God. According to Buber (1923), we may adopt two basic attitudes toward the world: *I-Thou* or *I-It*. *I-Thou* is a relation of subject-to-subject, but *I-It* is a relation of subject-to-object. In the *I-Thou* relation, we perceive each other as having a unity of being, rather than as consisting of isolated qualities. Thus, in an *I-Thou* relation, we engage in dialogue that mutually recognizes and affirms our whole being. In the *I-It* relation, on the other hand, we perceive each other as consisting of isolated qualities, and we perceive ourselves as part of a world that consists of things. *I-Thou* is a relation of mutuality and reciprocity, but *I-It* is a relation of remoteness and detachment.

We may try to convert the subject-to-subject relation into a subject-to-object relation, says Buber. However, the being of a subject is a unity that cannot be analyzed as an object. When a subject is analyzed as an object, the subject is no longer a subject and becomes an object. When a subject is analyzed as an object, the subject is no longer a *Thou* and becomes an *It*. The being that is analyzed as an object is the *It* in an *I-It* relation.

In a subject-to-subject relation, each subject affirms the other's unity of being. When a subject chooses or is chosen by the *I-Thou* relation, this act involves the subject's whole being. Thus, the *I-Thou* relation is an act of choosing or being chosen to become the subject of a subject-to-subject relation. The subject becomes a subject through the *I-Thou* relation, and the act of choosing this relation affirms the subject's whole being.

In the *I-Thou* relation, the *I* is unified with the *Thou*, says Buber. However, in the *I-It* relation, the *I* is detached from the *It*. In the *I-Thou* relation, the being of the *I* belongs to both *I* and *Thou*. In the *I-It* relation, however, the being of the *I* belongs to *I*, but not to *It*. *I-Thou* is a relation in which *I* and *Thou* have a shared reality. The *I* that has no *Thou* has a reality that is less complete than that of the *I* in the *I-and-Thou*. The more that *I-and-Thou* share their reality, the more complete is their reality.

For Buber, God is the eternal *Thou*, the only *Thou* who can sustain the *I-Thou* relation eternally. In the *I-Thou* relation between ourselves and God, there is a unity of being in which we can always find God. In the *I-Thou* relation, there is no barrier of other relations which separate us from God, and thus we can speak directly to God.

Chapter IV

DISCOURSE ANALYSIS

The Sign as a Linguistic Unit or Element

The term "semiotics" is derived from the Greek word *semeiotikos*, meaning "theory of signs." The term "semiosis," which refers to the process by which a sign-vehicle functions as a sign, is derived from the Greek word *semeiosis*, which refers to the action of signs. The Greek word *semeion* means "sign," "mark," or "token." *Semeion* (σημειον) is also the word which was used most frequently by New Testament writers as a term for "miracle."

A sememe is the smallest unit of meaning in a language. It may be the meaning expressed by a morpheme (the smallest grammatical or lexical unit of a language). Every sememe may be an element of a semantic field.

According to Umberto Eco (1979), every sign-vehicle has a position within a semantic field and may refer to other sign-vehicles within that particular field. A semantic field is the totality of sememes that may be expressed by a sign-vehicle (or word). A sign-vehicle may belong to more than one semantic field. Semantic fields may overlap and may be complementary, indifferent, or contradictory to each other. The semantic markers (semes) of a sememe are the positions which it may occupy within a semantic field. Denotative markers do not rely on a preceding denotation in order to constitute a sememe, but connotative markers rely on a preceding denotation in order to constitute a sememe. Sememes may be categorematic (having an independent meaning and being capable of standing on their own as subjects or predicates in a proposition), or they may be syncategorematic (having no independent meaning and being incapable of standing on their own as subjects or predicates in a proposition).

Algirdas Greimas (1979) describes sememes as consisting of nuclear semes and contextual semes (classemes). Nuclear semes are units of content on a content-plane which are correlated to units of expression (lexemes) on an expression-plane. Nuclear semes are not independent elements of meaning. They require contextual semes to establish their signification or meaning. Thus, they are also points of intersection between signifying relations. Classemes are semes whose recurrence (iterativity) along a syntagmatic chain establishes textual coherence and homogeneity. Classemes serve to disambiguate polysemes. Polysemes are semes (words or phrases) that have multiple meanings. For example, the polysemous noun "bark" may be disambiguated by the classeme (contextual seme) "rigging." The iterativity of classemes within a given text establishes the syntactic, semantic, or actorial isotopy of that particular text. The term "isotopy" refers to the number of readings or interpretations that are possible for a given text or unit of discourse. A simple isotopy consists of one possible reading, a bi-isotopy consists of two possible readings, and a pluri- or polyisotopy consists of many possible readings of a given word, text, or unit of discourse.

A grapheme is the smallest unit of writing in a language. It may be a letter, a punctuation mark, an ideogram, a numeral, or a symbol used to represent a phoneme (the smallest contrastive unit of sound in a language). Allographs are variant forms of a grapheme, which may be in complementary distribution, contrastive distribution, or free variation with respect to each other.

A lexeme is the fundamental unit of the lexicon (vocabulary) of a language. It is the smallest morphological unit that belongs to a particular syntactic category (e.g. noun, verb, adjective, adverb, etc.) and that has a semantic interpretation. For example, the verbs "speaks" and "speaking" are inflections (variations in form) of the lexeme "speak." The noun "speakers" is an inflection of the lexeme "speaker." The inflectional forms of a lexeme have paradigmatic relations to each other.

Text Semiotics

A message may occur within a text or may itself be a text. A text may be a manuscript, a book, a story, a newspaper, a televison program, an act of speech, a mode of nonverbal behavior, i.e. anything which can be studied semiotically. It may be a history, a religion, a culture, or a society.

Hypertext may also be a field of study for text semiotics. Hypertext is a computer-based information system in which blocks of text contain hyperlinks. Hyperlinks are automated links embedded in a block of text that allow the reader to select another block of text within the same document or to select another document. The user can navigate through a web of linked texts or documents. Navigation requires a browser (a computer program that allows the computer to display hypertext). "Hypermedia" is a term for multimedia hypertext, i.e. hypertext that contains plain text, visual images, audio, and video files. Hyperlinks may be embedded in visual images as well as in plain text, allowing the user to navigate freely through linked documents. HTML (hypertext markup language) is a set of codes that can be inserted into files in order to indicate how they are to be linked and how they are to be displayed

M.A.K. Halliday and Ruqaiya Hasan (1976) define a text as a linguistic unit characterized by cohesion and coherence. Cohesion is a semantic relation in which an element of a text depends for its interpretation on another element of the text. Cohesion may be expressed by exophoric or endophoric reference, by substitution, by ellipsis, by conjunction, and by lexical cohesion. Exophoric reference is extratextual or situational reference. Endophoric reference is intratextual reference, either anaphoric (referring to preceding text) or cataphoric (referrring to subsequent text). Substitution is replacement of one element by another. Ellipsis is omission of an element. Conjunction includes additive relations (e.g. "and"), adversative relations (e.g. "yet," "but," "however"), causal relations (e.g. "therefore," "consequently"), and temporal relations (e.g. "then," "finally").

Textuality is defined by both cohesiveness with respect to the text itself and coherence with respect to the contextual situation, according to Halliday and Hasan. The coherence of a text with respect to the contextual situation defines its consistency of register. The *register* of a text is its situational-semantic configuration, which has a *field*, *mode*, and *tenor*. The *field* is the total event in which the text functions, including the purposive activity of the speaker and the subject matter of the text. The *mode* is the function of the text in the total event, including the channel of communication, the genre of the text, and the rhetorical mode. The *tenor* is the set of relations among the participants involved.[1]

John Lyons (1995) agrees that in order for a sequence of utterances to be described as a text, it must have some cohesiveness of form and coherence of content. The structural units of a text must be connected in some way that is appropriate to the context.

Julia Kristeva (1980) defines a text as a trans-linguistic apparatus, because it transposes other texts into new arrangements and into new cultural or historical settings. A text is a kind of intertextuality in which other texts engage in dialogue. Every text is an intersection of other texts, and thus textual analysis is a trans-linguistic procedure.

Analysis of religious texts may be doctrinal, philological, historical, linguistic, or literary. Linguistic analysis is therefore only one of many possible methods of textual analysis. Analysis of texts as linguistic structures may include examination of their paradigms, syntagms, codes, use of rhetorical tropes (metonymy, synecdoche, metaphor, simile, irony, hyperbole, etc.), modes of articulation, and relations to other texts.

According to Roland Barthes (1988), textual analysis does not try to define the structure of a text. Its aim is not to determine the unity of the text, but to discover the rules according to which the text "explodes and disperses." Its aim is not to locate and classify all of the meanings in a text, but rather to discover the forms and codes according to which those meanings are possible.[2]

---

1. M.A.K. Halliday and Ruqaiya Hasan, *Cohesion in English* (Hong Kong: Longman Group Ltd., 1976), p. 22.

The syntagms of a text are the linear elements that form chains or strings. The paradigms of a text are the elements that may be substituted for each other in the same position within a given syntagmatic string. Greimas and Courtés (1979) explain that the syntagmatic axis is horizontal and that the paradigmatic axis is vertical. The syntagmatic axis is an axis of conjunctions and correlations, but the paradigmatic axis is an axis of disjunctions and commutations. The terms of a syntagmatic relation can be simultaneously present within a text, but the terms of a paradigmatic relation can only be substituted for each other.

The "commutation test" described by Barthes (1964) is a means of determining whether a given relation within a text is syntagmatic or paradigmatic. The test is performed by observing whether the reciprocal substitution of two signifiers produces a reciprocal substitution of two signifieds; if this occurs, then a syntagmatic relation between the pair of signifiers is present. Thus, the test determines whether a change in the plane of expression of a text produces a correlative change in the plane of its content.

The context in which linguistic utterances appear may be verbal or nonverbal. The verbal context may be intra- and intertextual, discursive, literary, and nonliterary. The nonverbal context may be social, psychological, cultural, and historical.

The non-literary verbal context of utterances may include informational, expository, procedural, and technical texts. The literary context may include novelistic, poetic, dramatic, critical, autobiographical, philosophical, religious, historical, and rhetorical texts. There may be overlap between different types of texts and textual contexts.

Foucault's Archaeology

Michel Foucault (1972) defines a discourse as any group of statements belonging to a single system of formation. It is also a group of statements whose rules of formation distinguish it from other groups of statements. The rules of formation of a discourse define not only its regularities, but also its thresholds, discontinuities, and limits.

Foucault defines a discursive formation as a system of dispersion between a group of statements, which has a regularity and order of its objects, forms, concepts, and themes. The formation of the objects of a discursive formation may be

---

2. Roland Barthes, "Textual Analysis: Poe's Valdemar," in *Modern Criticism and Theory: A Reader*, edited by David Lodge (London: Longham, 1988), p. 172.

determined by their "surfaces of emergence," their "authorities of delimitation," and their "grids of specification." The formation of the enunciative modalities of a discursive formation may be determined by the status of the discoursing subject, by the site from which the discoursing subject speaks, and by the position of the discoursing subject in relation to the various domains or groups of objects of the discursive formation. The formation of the concepts of a discursive formation may be determined by their "forms of succession," by their "forms of coexistence," and by their "procedures of intervention." The formation of the themes or strategies of a discursive formation may be determined by their "points of diffraction," "points of equivalence," and "points of systematization."

According to Foucault, a statement is a linguistic unit that is different from a sentence, a proposition, or an act of speech.[3] A statement is any series of signs that may appear in an enunciative field. Language may be regarded as a system for constructing possible statements.

The enunciative field of a statement may include the background of formulations in which the statement appears, and it may also include all of the situational and linguistic elements that are related to the statement and that determine its meaning. It may also include the formulations within which the statement appears and all of the formulations to which the statement refers. It may also include all of the formulations that are subsequently made possible by the statement.[4]

Every statement has an enunciative function that is independent of any subject who is making the statement. A statement is not merely a projection of signs onto a plane of language or an act of manipulating a set of linguistic elements.[5] A statement must have an associated enunciative field. The rules of formation for a discursive statement are also domains in which the statement operates as an enunciative function.

Foucault explains that a statement may not necessarily have the grammatical structure of a sentence or the logical structure of a proposition. However, a statement must have a *referent* (something to which it refers), a *subject* (a producer), an *associated field* (a domain of coexistence for other statements), and a *materiality* (a means through which it is expressed). While a sentence may belong to a text and a proposition may belong to a logical argument, a statement may belong to a discursive formation. Thus, the analysis of a discursive statement does not belong

---

3. Michel Foucault, *The Archaeology of Knowledge*, translated by A.M. Sheridan Smith (New York: Pantheon Books, 1972)., p. 86.
4. *Ibid.*, pp. 97-8.
5. *Ibid.*, p. 99.

to the same level of description as the analysis of a sentence or the analysis of a logical proposition. The enunciative level of a statement is different from the grammatical level of a sentence or the logical level of a proposition.

A discourse is a group of statements for which conditions of existence are definable, says Foucault. A discourse is also a historical event or an *archive* of historical statements. An archive is a system that governs the appearance of statements as historical events. The archive of a society, culture, or civilization is a system of formation (or of transformation) of statements, and it is characterized by discontinuity, because it tells us what we can no longer say. Thus, the description of any discursive formation is an archaeology.

The archaeological description of a discursive formation is not necessarily an attempt to interpret its meaning. Archaeological description is a method of discovering the rules that define the specificity of a discursive formation. Archaeological description does not attempt to describe the process by which a discoursing subject formulates an idea, and it does not attempt to explain the motives or intentions of the discoursing subject. Archaeological description is concerned with the rules that may be specific to discursive formations, and it is concerned with the rules that define discourse itself. According to Foucault, the enunciative modalities of discourse manifest the diversifying, rather than unifying, function of the speaking subject. Thus, archaeological description has a diversifying, rather than unifying, effect on our understanding of discursive statements.[6]

Bakhtin's Theory of Discourse

For Mikhail Bakhtin (1895-1975), an essential feature of any utterance is its addressivity (i.e. its quality of beng directed to an addressee). An utterance is a link in a chain of communicaton between an addresser and an addressee. Every utterance, however monological it may be, presupposes other utterances and must somehow take them into account. Thus, every utterance is in some way a response to previous utterances and is an invitation to subsequent utterances. Every utterance has a position within a given sphere of communication.[7]

---

6. The above discussion is from my chapter on Foucault in *The Conditions of Knowledge* (2006).
7. Mikhail Bakhtin, *The Bakhtin Reader,* edited by Pam Morris (London: Arnold, 1994), pp. 85-87.

While an isolated monologic utterance or an abstract system of linguistic signs may be an object of study for linguistics, says Bakhtin, the dialogic relations that may occur between utterances and between texts are fields of study for metalinguistics. Language is not merely a structured system of signs; it is a dialogic interaction between speakers and listeners, between addressers and addressees. While monological discourse is characterized by absolute point of view, univocality, and monophony, dialogical discourse is characterized by relativization of points of view, multivocality, and polyphony.

Bakhtin classifies discourse into three main types, based on its uni- or multivocality: 1) direct, unmediated discourse is unidirectional and univocal, and it is directed exclusively toward its referential object; 2) objectified or represented discourse objectifies or represents the discourse of someone other than the speaker (e.g. a character in a story or novel); and 3) double-voiced or multi-voiced discourse makes use of the discourse of someone other than the speaker by infusing it with the speaker's thoughts but nevertheless allowing it to express its own aspirations. Double-voiced discourse may be further divided into 1) unidirectional double-voiced discourse (including stylization, narrator's narration, and unobjectified discourse of a character who carries out the author's intentions), 2) varidirectional, double-voiced discourse (including parody, irony, and transmission of someone else's discourse with a shift in accent), and 3) active, reflected discourse of another speaker (including hidden internal polemic, hidden dialogue, rejoinder of a dialogue, and discourse that casts a sideward glance at someone else's word).[8]

According to Bakhtin, the relations between voices in a multi-voiced discourse may change with time, and the directional nature of discourse is dynamic. Monologue may become dialogue, and dialogue may become monologue. Monologic and dialogic relations may be combined within any given text or level of discourse.

Genette's Narrative Theory

Narrative theory (or narratology), as described by Gérard Genette (1988), is a theory of discourse that is concerned with narrative order, speed, frequency, mood, distance, perspective, focalization, voice, level, and other aspects of narrativity. Narrative theory analyzes the relations between a narrative and the events narrated, the relations between the narrative and the act of narration, the rela-

---

8. *Ibid.*, pp. 110-11.

tions between the narrator and the narrative, the relations between the narrator and the characters in a narrative, and the other intratextual relations of the narrative text itself

Genette takes a different viewpoint from Bakhtin in arguing that all narrative discourse is, to some extent, diagetic, because it is the retelling of an event or of a series of events. *Diagesis* is pure narration, without dialogue, as opposed to *mimesis*, which is dramatic representation. Thus, narration is a mode of "telling" rather than "showing."

According to Genette, a narrator's status in relation to a narrative may be 1) extradiagetic-heterodiagetic (if the narrator tells a story that she herself is absent from, i.e tells the story in the third-person), 2) extradiagetic-homodiagetic (if the narrator tells her own story in the first-person), 3) intradiagetic-heterodiagetic (if a character in a narrative tells a story that she is absent from, i.e. tells the story in the third-person), or 4) intradiagetic-homodiagetic (if a character in a narrative tells her own story in the first-person).

Similarly, "narratorial situations" may be described as 1) narratorial (authorial) third-person, 2) narratorial first-person, 3) figural third-person (if a character in a narrative tells a story that she is absent from), or 4) figural first-person (if a character in a narrative tells her own story).

The Generative Trajectory of Discourse

A.J. Greimas and J. Courtés (1979) use the term "generative trajectory" to describe the way in which discourse may proceed from simpler (more abstract) to more complex (more concrete) levels of production. According to their model, each of the various stages of discourse production has a syntactic and a semantic component. At the deepest or most abstract level of the generative trajectory, the semiotic and narrative structures of discourse have a deep level (which has a fundamental syntax and a fundamental semantics) and surface levels (which have a surface narrative syntax and a narrative semantics). At a higher and more concrete level, discursive structures have a discourse syntax (which governs actorialization, temporalization, and spatialization) and a discursive semantics (which governs thematization and figurativization). Textualization may intervene at any point in the generative trajectory.[9]

---

9. A.J. Greimas and J. Courtés, *Semiotics and Language: An Analytical Dictionary* (Bloomington: Indiana University Press, 1979), pp. 133-34.

The theory of a generative trajectory may be applied to generative syntactics as well as generative semantics. According to the theory of generative grammar developed by Noam Chomsky, the surface syntactic structure of sentences is not relevant to semantic interpretation, and the deep syntactic structure of sentences is not relevant to phonetic interpretation.[10] Greimas and Courtés therefore attempt to show that semantic interpretation may occur at various stages of the generative trajectory.

Chomsky's Generative Grammar

Chomsky (1965) makes a basic distinction between a speaker's knowledge of a language (or *competence*) and the speaker's actual use of language in concrete situations (or *performance*). This distinction is analogous to Saussure's distinction between *langue* and *parole*. A speaker's performance may not always reflect her actual competence, since she may become distracted while speaking, may have memory lapses, may have shifts of attention, etc. An adequate grammar of a language must therefore be able to assign structural descriptions to all of the statements that can be made or understood by an ideal speaker or listener.

Chomsky's generative grammar is based on the theory that an adequate grammar of a language should have both descriptive and explanatory adequacy, i.e. it should not only be able to provide structural descriptions of all statements that are made by a speaker but should also be able to provide structural descriptions of all statements that can possibly be made by a speaker. A descriptively-adequate grammar should therefore be able to correctly describe the competence of an ideal speaker or listener. A descriptively-adequate grammar should also be able to account for the generative capacity of language to create new phrase or sentence structures.

The model of a generative transformational grammar which Chomsky proposes in *Aspects of the Theory of Syntax* (1965) has three components: 1) a syntactic component, which generates the deep structures of sentences and then maps these deep structures into surface structures, 2) a semantic component which provides a semantic interpretation of the deep structures, and 3) a phonological component which provides a phonetic interpretation of the surface structures. The semantic and phonological components are purely interpretive and do not participate in the recursive generation of sentence structures (recursion is a property of syntactic rules whereby sentences structures can be embedded within each other).

---

10. *Ibid.*, p. 132.

According to Chomsky (1965), the syntactic component of a generative grammar has two subcomponents: 1) a set of base rules, and 2) a set of transformational rules. The base rules generate well-formed strings of syntactic elements, each string receiving an associated structural description called a base phrase-marker. These base phrase-markers are the elementary syntactic units of which deep structures are constituted.[11] The set of base rules, in turn, has two components: 1) a categorial subcomponent, which is a basic set of phrase-structure rules, and 2) a lexicon, which is an unordered list of all lexical formatives (minimal syntactically-functioning units). The rewriting rules of the categorial subcomponent determine the ordering of elements in deep structures.

The transformational rules of a generative grammar map deep structures into surface structures by assigning transformation markers to well-ordered strings of elements. The transformation markers specify operations to be performed on base phrase-markers (which are generated by the base rules).

Another model proposed by Chomsky (1980) attempts to identify more specifically the levels of generative grammar that are relevant to the semantic or phonetic interpretation of phrases or sentences. In contrast to the "standard model," this later model locates the semantic component of a generative grammar at the level of "S-structures" rather than "D-structures" (deep structures), although D-structures still play an important part in determining thematic relations. Base rules generate D-structures, which are converted by transformational rules into S-structures, which are then convertd into surface structures. S-structures are more abstract than surface structures, but they are relevant to phonetic interpretation because they can be mapped into surface structures. Transformational movement of elements from one structural level to another may leave behind phonetically-empty categories, which can be described by trace theory.

The Tasks of Discourse Analysis

Zelig Harris (1952), who was the first to describe discourse analysis as a field of study in linguistics, says that it is concerned not only with the role that syntactic elements play within the structure of individual sentences but also with the role that these elements play within the structure of texts. In contrast to descriptive linguistics, which is generally concerned with the elements of individual sentences, discourse analysis extends its field of study to the relations within (and

---

11. Noam Chomsky, *Aspects of the Theory of Syntax* (Cambridge: The M.I.T. Press, 1965), p. 17.

between) texts and the relations between language and culture (i.e. between linguistic and non-linguistic elements).

Discourse analysis may include the study of the stylistics, rhetoric, intertextuality, grammar, semantics, ideology, pragmatics, sociolinguistics, and psycholinguistics of a text or mode of discourse. Discourse analysis may also include genre theory and narrative theory (focusing on narrative viewpoint, structure, theme, mood, distance, level, and characterization).

Modes of religious discourse include theological discourse (including exegetical theology, historical theology, systematic theology, philosophical theology, and pastoral theology), liturgical discourse, ecumenical discourse, interfaith dialogue, canon law, scripture, sermonizing, preaching, prayer, confession, hymns, and chants.

Religious discourse may be instructional, testimonial, proclamatory, hortatory, evangelical, exegetical, admonitory, supplicatory, confessional, absolutory, or polemical in character. It may be monological (e.g. epic narrative) or dialogical (e.g. prayer). Monological and dialogical aspects of religious discourse may be combined and may supplement each other. For example, liturgy may be both monological (when it is read aloud) and dialogical (when a congregation delivers vocal or behavioral responses to a call to worship). Sermonizing may be both monological (when a preacher simply reads a sermon) and dialogical (when a preacher tries to actively engage his or her congregation).

Religious discourse may be combined with other modes of discourse, such as moral, legal, political, metaphysical, cosmological, or rhetorical discourse. Depending on historical and cultural context, these various modes of discourse may be compatible or incompatible with each other. Conflicts and inconsistencies may arise when religious discourse is presented as if it were scientific discourse or when political discourse is presented as it were religious discourse. There may be considerable controversy about the extent to which religious discourse should enter discourse concerning non-religious spheres of society.

The universe (or domain) of a particular religious discourse may include all of the signs (or words) in the discourse and all of the things that they signify (or represent). The universe of a religious discourse may also include all of the things that are stated or assumed by the discourse and all of the terms that are used in the discourse. Within the universe of all religious discourse (a macro-universe), there may be multiple universes (micro-universes); i.e. there may be multiple ways in which one can talk about God. Thus, the universe of all religious discourse may be a multiverse or megaverse, corresponding to the diversity of modes which it includes.

Todorov's Theory of Symbolism

Tzvetan Todorov (1974) describes linguistic symbolism as a mode of signification in which the meaning of the signified overflows the signifier. He distinguishes between three types of symbolism: 1) propositional, 2) lexical, and 3) graphic. In propositional symbolism, the meaning of a proposition is directly signified by a signifier, thereby leaving the proposition as a whole intact. In lexical symbolism, the meaning of a proposition is indirectly signified by a signifier, thereby leaving in abeyance the proposition as a whole. In graphic (or phonetic) symbolism, a proposition is segmented into its ultimate elements (words, sounds, letters), which become the signifiers of its meaning. An example of propositional symbolism is the story of Adam and Eve, presented as a real event and also as symbolically announcing the coming of Christ. An example of lexical symbolism is the same story presented as that of two particular human beings who symbolically represented all of humankind.

According to Todorov (1982), the interpretation of symbols may depend on their logical and linguistic structure, their direction of evocation, and their hierarchy of meanings. A sign or symbol may have both direct and indirect meanings, and it may have multiple ways of signifying those meanings. The primary meaning of a sign may depend on whether its direct meaning or indirect meaning is higher in the hierarchy. For example, *literal discourse* (i.e. discourse that signifies without evoking anything) has a higher level of direct meaning than indirect meaning. *Ambiguous discourse* has several direct meanings on exactly the same level, because of ambiguity of reference, polysemy of words, or ambiguity of illocutionary value. *Transparent discourse* has an obviously higher level of indirect meaning than direct meaning (e.g. euphemisms are transparent in meaning).[12]

The direct meaning of a sign may in some cases be contradictory to the indirect meaning of the sign. The indirect meaning of a sign may be grasped by the interpreter after the direct meaning of the sign has been grasped. The direct meaning of a sign may be verbally expressed at the same time that its indirect meaning is nonverbally expressed. The direct meaning of a sign may be determined by grammatical rules, while the indirect meaning of the sign may additionally be determined by context or setting.[13]

Todorov says that signs are "understood" but that symbols are "interpreted." The symbolics of language require the interpretation of indirect meanings. A text

---

12. Tzvetan Todorov, *Symbolism and Interpretation* (Ithaca: Cornell University Press, 1978), pp. 53-56.
13. *Ibid.*, p. 12.

or a discourse becomes symbolic when we discover through interpretation that it has an indirect meaning.[14]

Todorov also distinguishes between the term "language" and the term "discourse" by saying that discourse is a concrete manifestation of language produced within a specific context and having both linguistic and nonlinguistic elements (such as time and place at which it occurs, social setting, interpersonal relations between speaker and listener, etc.). An utterance is a segment of discourse which is produced by a speech act.[15]

Tagmemics

Tagmemics is a theory of discourse which was formulated by the American linguist Kenneth Pike, who proposed that discourse has three basic modes: phonology, lexicon, and grammar. Phonemes are basic phonetic units, morphemes are basic lexical units, and tagmemes are basic grammatical units. The grammatical structure of discourse consists of slots which can be filled by tagmemes. A tagmeme has four basic characteristics: 1) it has a *slot* or position in a structural setting, 2) it belongs to a *class* of items which are appropriately substitutable in the same slot, 3) it has a *role* or specific function in the structural setting, and 4) it has a *cohesion* to other grammatical units. These four characteristics of the tagmeme correspond to its syntagmatic, paradigmatic, pragmatic, and framework relations, respectively. Tagmemes, morphemes, and phonemes may be integrated into a grammatical, referential, and phonological hierarchy of words, phrases, clauses, and sentences.[16]

Biblical Rhetoric and Poetry

Biblical language is a literary and poetic language. It is written in verse, has a rhythmic structure, and makes use of poetic imagery. Literary forms in the Bible include parables (brief narratives that are designed to teach a moral lesson), allegories (longer narratives that are extended metaphors), proverbs (meaningful sayings or utterances), and psalms (sacred songs or hymns). The epistles are literary

---

14. *Ibid.*, p. 19.
15. *Ibid.*, p. 9.
16. David Crystal, *A Dictionary of Linguistics and Phonetics* (Oxford: Basil Blasckwell Ltd., 1980), p. 340.

letters to individuals or to groups of individuals (Romans, Corinthians, Galatians, etc).

Tremper Longman III (1993) explains that some of the literary conventions of biblical poetry include its terseness and compactness, its use of the line rather than the sentence as a basic struictural unit, its limited use of conjunctions, and its extensive use of parallelism in phrase and sentence structure. Other conventions of biblical poetry include its use of metaphor, figurative imagery, symbolism, and personification of inanimate objects. Longman also describes four principal types of poems that may be found in the Old Testament: lyric, epic, prophetic, and dramatic.[17]

Some of the rhetorical tropes used by New and Old Testament writers include *metaphor* ("I am the bread of life" John 6:35; "You are the salt of the earth" Matt. 5:13; "I am the Alpha and the Omega," Rev. 1:8; "So you, son of man, I have made a watchman for the house of Israel;" Ezek. 33:7), *simile* ("The kingdom of heaven is like treasure hidden in a field," Matt. 13:44, "Suddenly a sound came from heaven like the rush of a mighty wind," Acts 2:2), *synecdoche* ("Foreigners shall build up your walls, and their kings shall minister to you" (Isaiah 60:10), *metonymy* ("he who keeps Israel will neither slumber nor sleep" (Psalm 121:4), *irony* ("Why do you see the speck that is in your brother's eye, but do not notice the log that is in your own eye?" Matt. 7:3), and *hyperbole* ("it is easier for a camel to go through the eye of a needle than for a rich man to enter the kingdom of God," Matt. 19:24).

Other tropes commonly found in scriptural wrtings include *personification* (e.g. "O death, where is they victory? O death, where is thy sting?", 1 Cor. 15:55, which is also an example of *apostrophe*, i.e. a digression in the form of an address to someone not present or to a personified object or idea), *rhetorical questions* ("Am I not free? Am I not an apostle? Have I not seen Jesus our Lord?", 1 Cor. 9:1), and *paradox* ("Blessed are the meek, for they shall inherit the earth," Matt. 5:5; "The Lord giveth, and the Lord taketh away; blessed be the name of the Lord," Job 1:21).

Other examples of the use of paradox as a rhetorical trope in scriptural writings include the saying, "For whoever would save his life will lose it, and whoever loses his life for my sake and the gospel's will save it" (Mk. 9:35), and the saying

---

17. Tremper Longman III, "Biblical Poetry," in *A Complete Literary Guide to the Bible*, edited by Leland Ryken and Tremper Longman III (Grand Rapids: Zondervan Publishing House, 1993), pp. 80-91.

"If any one among you thinks that he is wise in this age, let him become a fool that he may become wise" (1 Cor. 3:18).

Another example of paradox is the sentence "But many that are first will be last, and the last first" (Mk. 10:31. This verse is also an example of *ellipsis* (the deliberate omission, for rhetorical effect, of a word or words implied by the context).

Rhetorical schemes used by New and Old Testament writers also include *parallelism* ("Ask, and it will be given you; seek, and you will find; knock, and it will be opened to you," Matt. 7:7), *apposition* ("I, Paul, a prisoner for Christ Jesus," Eph. 3:1), *anaphora* (repetition of the same word or group of words at the beginning of successive clauses, e.g. "whatever is true, whatever is honorable, whatever is just, whatever is pure, whatever is lovely, whatever is gracious, if there is any excellence, if there is anything worthy of praise, think about these things," 1 Phil. 4:80), *epistrophe* (repetition of the same word or group of words at the ends of successive clauses; e.g. "Love bears all things, believes all things, hopes all things, endures all things," 1 Cor. 13:7; "When I was a child, I spoke like a child, I thought like a child, I reasoned like a child," 1 Cor. 13:11), *polysyndeton* (the use of a number of conjunctions in close succession; e.g. "and a craftsman of any craft shall be found in thee no more; and the sound of the millstone shall be heard in thee no more; and the light of a lamp shall shine in thee no more; and the voice of bridegroom and bride shall be heard in thee no more" Rev. 22-23), and *antimetabole* (repetition in reverse order of words in successive clauses; e.g. "Whoever sheds the blood of man, by man shall his blood be shed," Gen. 9:6). Another rhetorical scheme, *asyndeton* (deliberate omission of conjunctions between successive clauses), is found in the *Gloria in Excelsis Deo* (hymn of praise): "we praise thee, we bless thee, we glorify thee, we give thanks unto thee."

Liturgical Language and Speech-act Theory

Liturgical language is different from colloquial language in its vocabulary, register, syntax, and semantic content. It incorporates biblical language, and it often contains archaisms. It also tends to be resistant to change. However, it has a number of performative functions. For example, it establishes a bond between the pastor and the congregation, and its recitation establishes the structural framework for a service of worship.

Speech-act theory may therefore be useful in analyzing the various functions of liturgical language. To recite the Lord's prayer is to perform the act of asking

God for help, guidance, and forgiveness. To say a prayer of thanksgiving is to perform the act of giving thanks to God.

J.L. Austin (1962) explains that acts of speech include constative utterances and performative utterances. Constative utterances report or describe something, but performative utterances do not report or describe anything. Constative utterances may be true or false, but performative uterances are neither true nor false. Performatives are nevertheless meaningful, because they are not merely acts of *saying* something but are acts of *doing* something. Thus, they may be "felicitious" (if they are properly invoked, applied, or executed) or "infelicitous" (if they are improperly invoked, applied or executed).

For example, the performative utterance "I apologize" is felicitious if the speaker is truly apologizing. The performative utterance "I believe in God, the Father almighty, maker of heaven and earth" is felicitous if the speaker truly believes in God, the Father almighty, maker of heaven and earth.

Austin distinguishes between three types of performative utterances: 1) locutionary acts, 2) illocutionary acts, and 3) perlocutionary acts. To perform a locutionary act is to perform an act of saying something. To perform an illocutionary act is to perform an act *in* saying something. To perform a perlocutionary act is to perform an act that is designed or intended to influence the feelings, thoughts, or actions of the listener, speaker, or other persons. To perform a locutionary act is also to perform an illoctuonary act.[18]

Performative utterances include acts of thanking, promising, apologizing, ordering, warning, sympathising, predicting, admitting, swearing, approving, disapproving, blaming, congratulating.

Austin divides performative utterances into five classes, according to their illocutionary force: 1) verdictives, 2) exercitives, 3) commissives, 4) behabitives, and 5) expositives. Verdictives give a verdict about something. Exercitives exercise powers, rights, or influence over someone or something. Commissives commit the speaker to doing something or declare an intention to do something. Behabitives are modes of social behavior, such as apologizing, sympathising, thanking, or congratulating. Expositives clarify the role of utterances in a monologue or dialogue.

Performative utterances may be explicit or implicit in the acts that they perform, says Austin, and thus constative utterances may actually be implicit performative utterances. The distinction between saying something and doing

---

18. J.L. Austin, *How to do things with Words* (Cambridge: Harvard University Press, 1962), p. 98.

something may ultimately not be able to be maintained, and all utterances may, in some way, be speech acts.

Speech devices which may function to increase the explicitness of performatives include 1) imperative mood or urgency, 2) tone of voice, 3) adverbs or adverbial phrases such as "probably" or "without fail," 4) connecting particles such as "although" or "moreover," 5) gestural or nonverbal accompaniments of an utterance, and 6) the circumstances of the utterance.[19] These are indicators of the "illocutionary force" of performatives, but Austin does not clearly define this term.

Illocutionary force is defined by Searle and Vanderveken (1985) as the combination of the "illocutionary point" of an utterance and the particular presuppositions accompanying that point (including the strength of the illocutionary point, the preparatory conditions, the propositional-content conditions, the mode of acheivement, and the strength of the sincerity conditions. The illocutionary point of an utterance is the basic purpose of the speaker in making the utterance.[20]

John R. Searle (1976) divides illocutionary acts into five main categories: 1) *representatives* (which, to varying degree, commit the speaker to the truth of the propositions they express), 2) *directives* (which, to varying degree, are attempts by the speaker to get the listener to do something, 3) *commissives* (which, to varying degree, commit the speaker to some future course of action), 4) *expressives* (which express the speaker's psychological response to a state of affairs specified in the propositional content of the utterance), and 5) *declarations* (which, if successfully performed, produce some alteration in the status of the thing or things to which they refer).[21]

Examples of commissive verbs include "ask," "request," "beg," "plead," "entreat," "pray," "invite," "permit," and "advise." Examples of expressive verbs include "thank," "congratulate," "apologize," "deplore," and "welcome."[22]

The speech acts performed during a service of religious worship thus include all of the kinds that Searle describes. Representative utterances include such statements as, "For the Lord is a great God, and a great King above all gods. In his hand are all the corners of the earth, and the strength of the hills is his also" (Psalm 95:3-4). Directive utterances include, "But thou, O Lord, have mercy

---

19. *Ibid.*, pp. 73-76.
20. John Searle and Daniel Vanderveken, *Foundations of Illocutionary Logic* (Cambridge: Cambridge University Press, 1985), pp. 7-21.
21. John R. Searle, "A classification of illocutionary acts," in *Language in Society*, Vol. 5 (1976), pp. 10-16.
22. *Ibid.*, pp. 10-16.

upon us, spare thou those who confess their faults, restore thou those who are penitent." Commissive utterances include such statements as "I will sing to the Lord, for he is lofty and uplifted, the horse and its rider has he hurled into the sea" (Exodus 15:1). Expressive utterances include, "We do earnestly repent, and are heartily sorry for these our misdoings." And declarations include., "From this day all generations will call me blessed: the Almighty has done great things for me, and holy is his Name."[23]

James H. Ware, Jr. (1981) explains that there are at least four kinds of liturgical speech acts: 1) enabling, 2) relational, 3) directive, and 4) exalting. Enabling speech acts include acts of blessing, cleansing, forgiving, fortifying, assuring, revealing, transforming, or imputing significance. Relational speech acts include acts of calling, thanking, promising, covenanting, confessing, communing, ordaining, interceding, invoking, greeting, or dedicating. Directive speech acts include acts of commanding, advising, teaching, charging, or instructing. Exalting speech acts include acts of praising, honoring, glorifying, adoring, rejoicing, or magnifying. All of these speech acts are processes of participatory communion with God. Each has its own unique objectives and grammars, and all are mutually complementary.[24]

The level of formality of liturgical language may be increased by the presence of archaic expressions such as "thou" and "takest." Examples of archaisms include "For thou only art holy, Thou only art the Lord," and "O ye heavens, bless ye the Lord." The vocative case is more frequently used in liturgical language than in contemporary language e.g. "O Lord, open thou my lips, and my mouth shall show forth thy praise" (Psalm 51:15). Revisions of the liturgy have periodically been made by the Church in order to prevent archaic language from becoming a barrier to communication.

---

23. *The Book of Common Prayer* (Oxford: Oxford University Press, 1979), pp. 37-60, 75-102.
24. James H. Ware, Jr., *Not with Words of Wisdom: Performative Language and Liturgy* (Washington, D.C.: University Press of America, 1981), pp. 40-46.

Chapter V

CHRISTIAN SEMIOTICS IN ART AND LITERATURE

Architecture

Christian semiotics has played an important role in the history of literature and the arts. The earliest examples prior to the Middle Ages included catacomb frescos and Byzantine iconography. Later examples included mosaics and medieval illuminated manuscripts.

In architecture, the most obvious examples of Christian semiotics include medieval Gothic cathedrals, such as Rheims, Chartres, Notre Dame, Toledo, Siena, Pisa, Köln, and Salisbury.

Characteristic architectural features of Gothic cathedrals include huge dimensions with soaring edifices, pointed arches, ribbed vaults, and flying buttresses. Multiple stained-glass windows are usually present, and there may be a tympanum (or sculpted panel) above the main entrance of a cathedral, along with other exterior sculptural effects (such as gargoyles).

Interior architectural components of a typical Gothic-style church or cathedral include 1) the *nave* (the central longitudinal area where the congregation is seated on rows of pews, divided by a central aisle and flanked on each side by narrower aisles), 2) the *narthex* (the vestibule between the main entrance and the nave), 3) the *chancel* or *sanctuary* (the altar space enclosed by a railing), 4) the *transepts* (the transverse extensions which cross the nave at the entrance to the chancel, forming a cross-shaped floor plan), 5) the *choir* (the part of the chancel reserved for the singers), 6) the *lectern* (the speaker's stand from which the lessons are read), 7) the *pulpit* (the elevated platform from which the preacher delivers a sermon), 8) the *cathedra* (the seat or throne on which a bishop sits in the chancel), 9) the *sacristy* (the room adjacent to the sanctuary where the sacred vessels and clerical vestments are stored), 10), the *vestry* (the room where the choir and clergy change their vestments), 11) the *apse* (the vaulted semicircular recess at the end of the choir), and 12) the *clerestory* (the portion of the interior rising above the nave and transepts). There may be galleries or arcades along each each side of the clerestory.

Symbolism in church architecture may include biblical scenes on sculpted panels, scenes from the life of Christ on stained glass windows, exterior statuary portraying saints or angels, and interior paintings or decorations with religious themes.

Richard Kieckheffer (2004) suggests that when we enter a church, we are also entering into a spiritual process and into the presence of the sacred. A church can be a dramatic setting for the interplay of immanence and transcendence, giving us a sense of participation in a reality greater than ourselves. Church architecture may inspire a sense of awe, of mystery, and of timelessness.[1] Such factors as lighting, height, and acoustics may convey particular aesthetic qualities that contribute to the experience of worship. The longitudinal spatial dynamics of a church invite processional movement, and they may signify progression from one stage to another in the service of worship.[2]

Painting

In painting, examples of Christian semiotics include the paintings of Giotto, Duccio, Jan Van Eyck, Fra Angelico, Andrea Mantegna, Sandro Botticelli, Leonardo da Vinci, Giovanni Bellini, Pietro Perugino, Giorgione, Michelangelo, and Raphael. Other examples include the biblical scenes depicted by such artists as Hieronymus Bosch, Giorgio Vasari, Paolo Veronese, El Greco, Caravaggio, Guercino, Rembrandt van Rijn, Francisco de Zurburan, Bartolomé Esteban Murillo, William Blake, Thomas Eakins, Henry Ossawa Tanner, Egon Schiele, Lovis Corinth, Salvador Dali, and Graham Sutherland.

Sculpture

In sculpture, examples of Christian semiotics incude the biblical figures depicted by such artists as Claus Sluter, Tilman Riemenschneider, Lorenzo Ghiberti, Donatello, Michelangelo, Gian Lorenzo Bernini, Auguste Rodin, Constantin Brancusi, and Jacob Epstein.

Poetry

In poetry, the quest for spiritual salvation has been explored by such writers as Dante Alighieri, Geoffrey Chaucer, Edmund Spenser, John Donne, John Milton, Richard Crashaw, William Blake, Samuel Taylor Coleridge, Johann Wolfgang von Goethe, Emily Dickinson, Alfred, Lord Tennyson, Gerard Manley Hopkins, Rainer Maria Rilke, T.S. Eliot, and W.H. Auden.

---

1. Richard Kieckhefer, *Theology in Stone: Church Architecture from Byzantium to Berkeley* (Oxford: Oxford University Press, 2004), p. 103.
2. *Ibid.*, p. 25.

Fiction

In modern fiction, the nature of sin and redemption has been explored by such writers as Fyodor Dostoyevsky, Leo Tolstoy, Nathaniel Hawthorne, Herman Melville, Thomas Mann, Ignazio Silone, Graham Greene, William Faulkner, and Flannery O'Connor. Other writers whose work has been strongly influenced by Christian themes include Anthony Trollope and C.S. Lewis.

Drama

In drama, the passion plays of the thirteenth to sixteenth centuries were reenactments of the crucifixion and resurrection of Jesus. The miracle plays of the thirteenth to sixteenth centuries portrayed miracles of the Virgin Mary and the Saints. Dramatists since the sixteenth century whose works have reflected Christian themes include Christopher Marlowe, Jean Racine, Friedrich Schiller, August Strindberg, T. S. Eliot, Eugene O'Neill, George Bernard Shaw (who was an avowed atheist), Arthur Miller, Christopher Durang, and John Patrick Shanley.

Music

In music, Christian rites of worship have been the subject of such majestic and inspiring works as J.S. Bach's *Mass in B Minor*, Wolfgang Amadeus Mozart's *Requiem Mass*, G.F. Handel's *Messiah*, and Johannes Brahms' *German Requiem*. Other requiems have been composed by Hector Berlioz, Giuseppe Verdi, Gabriel Fauré, Antonin Dvorák, Frederick Delius, and Benjamin Britten. The *Te Deum Laudamus* (*Hymn of Thanksgiving*) has been set to music by many composers, including Henry Purcell, G.F. Handel, Hector Berlioz, Giuseppe Verdi, Antonin Dvorák, Anton Bruckner, Ralph Vaughn Williams, Benjamin Britten, and Sir William Walton.

Film

In film, dramatizations of the life of Jesus have included *The King of Kings* (directed by Cecil B. DeMille, 1927), *King of Kings* (Nicholas Ray, 1961), *The Greatest Story Ever Told* (George Stevens, 1965), *Il Vangelo secondo Matteo* (*The Gospel According to Saint Matthew*, Pier Paolo Pasolini, 1966), *Jesus Christ Superstar* (Norman Jewison, 1973), *Godspell* (David Greene, 1973), *Jesus of Nazareth*

(Franco Zeffirelli, 1977), *The Last Temptation of Christ* (Martin Scorsese, 1988), and *The Passion of the Christ* (Mel Gibson, 2004)

Biblical themes have also inspired such films as *Samson and Delilah* (Cecil B. DeMille, 1949), *Quo Vadis* (Mervyn Leroy, 1951, based on the novel by Henryk Sienkiewicz), *The Robe* (Henry Koster, 1953), *The Ten Commandments* (Cecil B. DeMille, 1956), *Ben-Hur* (William Wyler, 1959, based on the novel by Lew Wallace), and *Barabbas* (Richard Fleischer, 1962).

Christian themes have also inspired such films as *The Song of Bernardette* (directed by Henry King, 1943, *Black Narcissus* (Michael Powell and Emeric Pressburger, 1947), *A Man Called Peter* (Henry Koster, 1955), *The Nun's Story* (Fred Zinneman, 1959), *Elmer Gantry* (Richard Brooks, 1960), *The Cardinal* (Otto Preminger, 1963), *Lillies of the Field* (Ralph Nelson, 1963), *The Shoes of the Fisherman* (Michael Anderson, 1968, based on the novel by Morris West), *Rosemary's Baby* (Roman Polanski, 1968), *The Exorcist* (William Friedkin, 1973, based on the novel by William Peter Blatty), *The Omen* (Richard Donner, 1976), *Dead Man Walking* (Tim Robbins, 1995, based on the book by Sister Helen Prejean), and *The Da Vinci Code* (Ron Howard, 2006, based on the novel by Dan Brown).

Christian Aesthetics

All of the various genres of art and literature may be fields of study for semiotic aesthetics. According to Charles W. Morris (1971), semiotic aesthetics is concerned with the composition, meaning, uses, purposes, and functions of aesthetic signs.

Semiotic aesthetics may include a theory of art, a theory of aesthetic activity, a theory of the nature of aesthetic qualities, a theory of interpretation, and a theory of aesthetic codes.. A work of art may be viewed as a sign, as a sign element, or as a system of signs. To experience a work of art may be to experience a set of aesthetic signs.

Christian aesthetics, from a semiotic standpoint, is a study of aesthetic signs or values. If Christianity is a language of faith, then Christian aesthetics may be a study of the art of that language. The language of art may be a language of signs and symbols.

Correggio's *Ecce Homo*

A noteworthy example of Christian semiotics in art is Correggio's painting *Ecce Homo* (*Christ Presented to the People*, 1525-30), which is in the permanent collection of the National Gallery, London. It is based on the biblical scene in which Pilate presents Jesus to the people before the crucifixion. Jesus has been scourged, and the soldiers have placed a crown of thorns on his head. Pilate says to the people, "Here is the man!" (*Ecce Homo*, in Latin). When the chief priests and the crowd see Jesus, they cry out, "Crucify him, crucify him!" And Pilate says to them, "Take him yourselves and crucify him, for I find no crime in him" (John 19:1-6).

Antonio Allegri da Correggio (c. 1494-1534) was an Italian painter who was born in Correggio, near Parma, and who did much of his work in Parma. He decorated the dome of the Church of San Giovanni Evangelista in Parma (1520-24) with a painting of St. John ascending to heaven, and he decorated the dome of the cathedral of Parma (1526-30) with a painting of the Assumption of the Virgin Mary.. His other well-known paintings include *Venus and Cupid with a Satyr* (Louvre, Paris), *The Education of Cupid* (National Gallery, London), *The Nativity* (Staatiche Kunstsammlungen, Dresden), *Christ Appearing to Mary Magdeleine in the Garden* (*Noli Me Tangere*, Prado Museum, Madrid), *Deposition* (Galleria Nazionale, Parma), *Martyrdom of Four Saints* (Galleria Nazionale, Parma), and *Ganymede* (Kunsthistorisches Museum, Vienna).

Correggio, *Christ Presented to the People* (*Ecce Homo*), probably about 1525-30, oil on poplar, 99.7 x 80 cm., National Gallery of Art, London.

Correggio's *Ecce Homo* shows Jesus being handed over by Pilate to the people for crucifixion. Jesus is at the center of the paintng, with Pilate to his right, a soldier to his left, and the Blessed Virgin Mary at his side. She is swooning in dismay. Jesus has a crown of thorns on his head and a robe draped around his shoulders. His chest is bare, and his wrists are bound. He has a look of sorrow on his face, contemplating human willfulness and iniquity. His expression reveals resignation, compassion, and self-sacrifice. As Isaiah 53:3 says, "He was despised and rejected by men; a man of sorrows, and acquainted with grief; and as one from whom men hide their faces he was despised, and we esteemed him not."

In the painting, Jesus is mocked by the soldier who leans toward him and whose dark countenance suggests evil and corruption. Pilate to his right is looking not at Jesus but at the viewer. Pilate is holding up his right hand, indicating that here is the man who has been accused and that here is a lession which should be learned. The scene is made even more powerful by the fact that Jesus is suffering for us despite his own blamelessness.

Correggio has arranged the hands of the figures in the painting in various poses. The hands of all of the figures have a remarkable gentleness and delicacy. The robes of Jesus and of Pilate have a lush, flowing, warm color and tone. The skin of Jesus' chest and arms has a radiant translucency, and the gentleness with which his hands are posed reveals his innocence, his acceptance of his role as redeemer and his submission to the will of God. He is like a lamb led to the slaughter, and humankind, in mocking and despising him, is like a flock that has gone astray. "He was wounded for our transgressions, he was bruised for our iniquities, upon him was the chastisement that made us whole, and with his stripes we are healed" (Isaiah 53:5).

The scourging of Christ has been the subject of paintings by many artists. Other artists who have produced works entitled *Ecce Homo* include Antonello da Messina, Quentin Massys, Heironymus Bosch, Hans Holbein, Titian, Caravaggio, Peter Paul Rubens, Anthony van Dyck, Rembrandt van Rijn, Jusepe de Ribera, Bartolomé Esteban Murillo, Lovis Corinth, and Georges Rouault. Prints entitled *Ecce Homo* have been produced by Albrecht Dürer, Martin Schongauer, Honoré Daumier, and James Ensor.

Milton's *Paradise Lost*

In poetry, an outstanding example of Christian semiotics is John Milton's *Paradise Lost* (1667). It is widely regarded as the greatest epic poem in English literature, and it is remarkable not only for its cosmic sweep, rhetorical eloquence, and dramatic scale, but also for its comprehensive treatment of a wide range of themes which are central to Christianity.

John Milton (1608-1674) was an English poet who was born in London. He was the oldest of three children born to John and Sarah Milton. His father was a scrivener (notary and businessman) as well as a musician and composer. Milton attended St. Paul's School in London from 1620-1625. He entered Christ College, Cambridge in 1625, but he was expelled the next year because of an altercation with his tutor, William Chappell. However, he was readmitted later that same year and was able to obtain a new tutor, Nathaniel Tovey. Milton graduated with a B.A. from Cambridge in 1629, and he continued his studies there, receiving an M.A. in 1632. After leaving Cambridge, he lived with his parents in London and devoted himself to writing poetry, producing some of his most famous works, including *L'Allegro* (1632), *Il Pensero* (1632), *Comus* (a masque,

1634), and *Lycidas* (an elegy, 1637). In 1638-9, he traveled to France, Italy, and Switzerland, and after returning to London, he became a teacher to his nephews, John and Edward Phillips. In 1642, with the outbreak of the English Civil War, Milton supported the Puritan cause by writing a number of pamphlets attacking episcopacy (the government of the church by bishops). In 1642, at the age of 33, he married 17-year-old Mary Powell. Their marriage was unhappy, and a few months after they were married, she returned to live with her parents in Oxfordshire. Milton subsequently wrote a series of controversial pamphlets on the subject of divorce. In 1645, Mary, whose family had supported the Royalists and had been forced to leave Oxfordshire after the Royalist defeat at the Battle of Naseby, returned to Milton in London, accompanied by her whole family. In 1646, Mary's first child, Anne, was born. In 1648, a second child, Mary, was born. In 1649, King Charles I was executed, and Milton was appointed Secretary of Foreign Tongues to the Council of State. This was a post in which he handled diplomatic correspondence, principally in Latin. In 1651, Mary's third child, John, was born. In 1652, Milton became completely blind. On May 2, Mary's fourth child, Deborah, was born, but Mary died three days later, and their infant son John died in June. In 1656, Milton married Katherine Woodcock, but she died two years later. In 1657, the poet Andrew Marvell was appointed Milton's assistant. In 1660, the monarchy was restored, and Milton was dismissed from office, arrested, fined, and then released. In 1663, he married 24-year-old Elizabeth Minshull. His masterpiece, *Paradise Lost*, was published in 1667, followed by a sequel, *Paradise Regained*, in 1671, and his dramatic poem, *Samson Agonistes*, was published in 1671. He died in 1674 and was buried next to his father in St. Giles Churchyard, Cripplegate, London. He was survived by his wife and three daughters. His last known descendant, Elizabeth Foster, died in 1754.

Milton had a complex personality that combined elements of Puritanism, austerity, self-discipline, idealism, pride, and ambition.[3] He was harsh in his treatment of his daughters, who had to act as readers and scribes for him after he lost his sight, and they left home to live on their own after he married Elizabeth Minshull.

In his treatise, *De Doctrina Christiana* (*On Christian Doctrine*, unpublished until 1823), Milton divides Christian doctrine into two realms: 1) faith (or knowledge of God) and 2) love (or worship of God). Comprehensive knowledge of God is beyond the capability of the human intellect, says Milton, but God has revealed himself to us as fully as we are capable of understanding. The existence

---

3. *Benét's Reader's Encyclopedia* (New York: Harper & Row, 1987), p. 652.

of God is proved to us by own own reasoning, because if there were no God, then there would be no difference between right and wrong, between virtue and vice, or between good and evil. That there are, in fact, such differences is proof of God's existence. There is only one true God (John 17:3), and he is a living God (John 17:3; 1 Thess. 1:9). God is infinite, eternal, immutable, omnipotent, omnipresent, omniscient, just, faithful, and gracious. God has given all mankind the power of free will. Thus, God had foreknowledge that Adam would fall of his own free will. Adam's fall was certain, but not necessary. God has predestined to salvation all those who believe in him and who have faith. God is just, and there is no one to whom he does not offer sufficient grace for salvation. God excludes no one from being redeemed by love and faith.

In *De Doctrina Christiana*, Milton also rejects the doctrine of the Trinity. He says that the Son (prior to being incarnated as Jesus) was "begotten of" (created by) the Father, and that therefore the Son is not coeternal with the Father. The Father had the power to create the Son, and the Son is therefore not coequal with the Father. After the Father created the Son, the Son created the universe, and the Son is not the same as the Father, says Milton. The Father alone is God, and he is a single person, not three persons.

Paradise Lost tells the story of Adam and Eve, their temptation by Satan, their disobedience to God's commandment not to eat the fruit of the tree of knowledge, and their ultimate expulsion from the Garden of Eden. It is written in blank verse and is divided into twelve books. Each book begins with a section in prose entitled "The Argument," which summarizes the events of the story. The verse is written in long paragraphs, which are the basic structural units of the poem.

The main characters are Adam and Eve, God the Father, the Son of God (the Messiah), the holy angels (Michael, Gabriel, Raphael, Abdiel, and Uriel), Satan (or Lucifer), the fallen angels (Beelzebub, Moloch, Belial, Mammon, and Mulciber), and Satan's offspring, Sin and Death.

Adam has been created in the image of God, and as such he is the father of all humankind. Created from a handful of dust and formed into a noble shape, he was given life when God breathed into his nostrils (VII, 525). Having been created free, he is free to act rightly or wrongly, to obey or disobey God. His natural instinct is to obey God, but he gradually realizes that he has the freedom to obey or disobey. He seeks knowledge of his past as well as of his future, and thus he asks the archangel Raphael to tell him the story of how the world was created (Book VII).

Eve has been formed from one of Adam's ribs into a being with whom he shares life in paradise. She is beautiful, gentle, sweet, and innocent. She is also submissive and compliant to Adam's will. She and Adam are two interdependent beings. Adam realizes that she is "Bone of my Bone, Flesh of my Flesh, my Self before me" (VIII, 495-6). He also realizes that they are "one Flesh, one Heart, one Soul" (VIII, 499). Thus, Satan is only able to approach Eve when she and Adam are separately caring for the garden. Satan perceives that she is more vulnerable to his fraud and deceit. She is less circumspect than Adam and is less firm of will. Thus, Satan is finally able to persuade her to eat the forbidden fruit of the tree of knowledge.

Satan is the most fully-developed character in the poem, and he is the central figure of Books I and II. He is the leader and mastermind of the fallen angels in hell. After having led a failed revolt against God, he has been cast with his minions into a dismal abyss. He is envious of God's power and is ambitious to attain a position of glory above his own peers. He hopes to avenge his defeat by subverting God's creation of paradise.

According to Satan, it is "better to reign in Hell, than serve in Heav'n" (Book I, 263). He regards power as an end in itself, and in his view, any means of attaining power is justified. He is a schemer and deceiver, and he is tormented by both his lost happiness and the continuing pain of living in hell.

God is portrayed in the poem as a holy light, and heaven is described as a realm of light. God sits on a throne in heaven, ruling the universe with justice and wisdom. He has acted benevolently by creating Adam and Eve sufficiently able to withstand temptation but free to act according to their own will. He is an "Omnipotent, Immutable, Immortant, Infinite, Eternal King," and he is the "Author of all being" (III, 373-4).

The Son of God sits at the right hand of the Father. He is exalted above all names in heaven and on earth. He epitomizes filial obedience, divine compassion, unending love, and grace without measure (III, 142-3). When God foretells the fall of Adam and Eve, the Son offers himself as a ransom in order to redeem humankind. God ordains the incarnation of his Son, and he commands all of the angels to adore him. In Book VII, Raphael also says that God sent the Son to create the world in six days.

Other important characters in the poem include Sin and Death. Sin is Satan's daughter, born from his head without a mother. She is a woman from the waist up and a serpent from the waist down. Around her waist is a pack of hellhounds who have their kennel in her womb. Death is a dark and dreadful monster who brandishes a dart. He is a gruesome fiend who raped his mother, and the hellhounds are their offspring.

Book I presents Satan and the other fallen angels in Hell, where they are in a place of darkness called Chaos. Satan tells his legions of a new world which is to be created by God according to a prophesy in heaven. To find out the truth of this prophesy and to decide what to do, Satan calls forth a full council. Pandemonium, the palace of Satan, rises suddenly out of the deep.

In Book II, Satan tells the council that he will undertake the journey to the new world. He travels to the gates of hell, which are guarded by his daughter, Sin, and by the son of their incestuous union, Death. Satan persuades Sin and Death to open the gates of hell, and he then continues his journey.

In Book III, God sees Satan traveling toward the newly created world. God foretells the success of Satan in tempting Adam and Eve. Although they will be seduced by Satan and will yield to temptation, God offers them grace, because their fall did not arise from malice on their own part, as did the fall of Satan. However, God declares that grace cannot be extended to mankind without the satisfaction of divine justice. Adam and Eve will offend the majesty of God by aspiring to be equal to God, and therefore they will have to die unless someone can be found who can sufficiently answer for their offense and undergo their punishment. The Son of God freely offers himself as a ransom for humankind, and God accepts his offer. Meanwhile, Satan travels to the orb of the sun and disguises himself as an angel. He is able to learn from Uriel (a holy angel who is regent of the sun) where the new world is located.

In Book IV, Satan arrives at Eden and disguises himself in the shape of a cormorant, sitting on the tree of life. He beholds Adam and Eve and resolves to bring about their downfall. He overhears them talking to each other, and he learns that the fruit of the tree of knowledge is forbidden to them, under penalty of death. Meanwhile, Uriel, having noted Satan's agitated gestures on the mount near Eden, warns Gabriel that an evil spirit has escaped from the deep and has disguised itself as a good angel. Gabriel confronts Satan, and Satan flies out of paradise.

In Book V, God sends Raphael to warn Adam about Satan, thereby making Adam inexcusable for disobedieince to the commandment not to eat the fruit of the tree of knowledge. Raphael tells Adam the story of Satan's revolt in heaven, and in Book VI he tells how Michael and Gabriel were sent forth into battle against Satan and the rebelling angels. On the third day of the tumult, God sent his Son, for whom the glory of victory was reserved, into battle, driving in a chariot with thunder. Satan's army was driven from heaven and fell to a place of punishment which had been prepared for them in the deep.

In Book VII, Raphael, at the request of Adam, tells him how the new world was created.

In Book VIII, Adam tells Raphael what he remembers of his life in paradise, of his talk with God concerning solitude, and of the creation of Eve. Raphael again warns Adam to beware of temptation, and he then departs.

In Book IX, Satan takes the form of a serpent and tempts Eve to eat the fruit of the tree of knowledge. She finally yields and eats the fruit. When she brings the fruit to Adam and tells him how she was persuaded to eat, he is dismayed. Perceiving that she is lost and that she will perish, he decides, because of his love for her, that he will perish with her. He takes the fruit from her, and he eats. Having lost their innocence, they discover that they are naked, and they try to cover their nakedness with leaves from a fig tree. Then they quarrel with each other.

In Book X, God sends his Son to judge Adam and Eve. Sin and Death leave the gates of hell, and they pave a broad highway over Chaos as they come to earth. Satan returns to the palace of Pandemonium in hell, where he and his legions are suddenly transformed by God into serpents and are punished with thirst and hunger.

In Book XI, the Son of God presents to his Father the prayers of the repentant Adam and Eve, thereby interceding for them. God accepts their repentance, but he declares that they can no longer live in paradise. Michael is sent to lead Adam and Eve from paradise. Michael tells Adam the story of humankind, up until the time of the flood. In Book XII, Michael continues the story and tells Adam about Abraham, Moses, and the coming of the Messiah. Then Michael leads Adam and Eve out of paradise.

A central theme of *Paradise Lost* is that of Adam and Eve's disobedience to the will of God and of their salvation through faith in God. Raphael says to Adam, "That thou art happy, owe to God; That thou continu'st such, owe to thyself, That is, to thy obedience" (V, 521-3). Obedience to God's will gives us the strength to resist temptation. Disobedience causes our fall from grace. The price for disobedience is misery. "With Satan, he who envies now thy state,/Who now is plotting how he may seduce/Thee also from obedience, that with him/Bereav'd of happiness thou mayst partake/His punishment, Eternal misery" (VII, 900-04).

For Milton, obedience is that of son to father, of wife to husband, and of humankind to God. There is a moral order in the universe according to which human beings must obey natural and divine law. The natural order of things is for God's will to be obeyed, and disobedience leads to catastrophe. Freedom is obedience to reason: "God left free the Will, for what obeys Reason is free" (IX, 351-2).

Other themes of the poem include the oppositions between good and evil, light and darkness, heaven and hell, order and chaos, law and anarchy, submission and revolt, love and hate, redemption and sin, forgiveness and revenge, mercy and punishment.

Of all the characters in the poem, Satan is given the most attention by the poet and is described in greatest detail. Satan's motivation to subvert the innocence of Adam and Eve is complex. He has, first of all, a lust for power: "To reign is worth ambition though in Hell," he says to the other fallen angels (I, 263). Although he hates having to submit to God's power, he wants to exercise the same degree of power over the universe. He feels envy, anger, and despair (IV, 115). He is jealous of the Son who has been proclaimed Messiah (V, 662-3). He is contemptuous of the archangel Gabriel, because the latter is obedient to God: "Ride on thy wings, and thou with thy Compeers,/Us'd to the yoke," (IV, 974-5), he says.

Satan is "the adversary of God and Man" (II, 629). He intends to reascend from Hell and to become monarch over Heaven. "For who can yet believe, though after loss,/That all these puissant Legions, whose exile/Hath emptied Heav'n, shall fail to re-ascend/Self-rais'd, and repossess their native seat?" (I, 631-4) he says to his minions. He sits on a throne in Hell, just as God sits on a throne in Heaven. He attempts to emulate God, and he inspires awe among the other fallen angels. However, his pride and ambition are his downfall. He is "insatiate to pursue/Vain War with Heav'n" (II, 8-9), but he fails to learn from his errors. God's victory is clearly inevitable (II, 769-70). Divine will cannot be thwarted or contravened.

Unable to oppose God's will by force, Satan uses fraud and deception instead. "Our better part remains/To work in close design, by fraud or guile/What force effected not" (I, 645-7), he says. Strategies which he employs in order to tempt Eve to eat the forbidden fruit include flattery, telling her of the sweetness of the fruit and of its power to increase the capacity for reasoning, pretending to admire and to feel a sense of loyalty toward her, denying that the fruit will cause death (as God has told her), falsely claiming to have himself already eaten of the fruit, telling her that God will not care whether she disobeys the comandment not to eat the fruit, telling her that God's commandment not to eat the fruit is merely a strategy on the part of God to keep her ignorant and lowly, telling her that knowledge of good and evil will make her a god, telling her that she cannot be harmed by having knowledge, and telling her that there is nothing wrong with eating the fruit if it brings knowledge and wisdom.

There are many parallelisms within the structure of the poem. Hell is a realm of darkness, while Heaven is a realm of light. Hell is also a realm of chaos, while Heaven is a realm of order. Sin holds the keys to the gates of hell, while Saint Peter holds the keys to the gates of heaven. Chaos is "umpire" in hell (II, 907), while conscience is "umpire" in heaven (III, 195). Satan is the father of Sin, while God is the Father of the Son. The fallen archangels Beelzebub, Moloch, Belial, and Mammon have their counterparts in the holy archangels Michael, Raphael, Gabriel, Abdiel, and Uriel.

Sin and Death are interdependent, just as Adam and Eve are interdependent. Sin has given birth to Death, and Death does not devour Sin because of his fear that her death would be his own (II, 805-8).

Hell is described as both a physical and a mental reality. "The mind is its own place, and in itself/Can make a Heav'n of Hell, a Hell of Heav'n" (I,254-5), says Satan to the other fallen angels. Later, after Adam and Eve have eaten the fruit and they start quarreling with each other about who should accept blame for their disobedience to God, their mutual accusations disrupt the tranquility of paradise. "High winds worse within/Began to rise, high Passions, Anger, Hate,/Mistrust, Suspicion, Discord, and shook sore/Their inward state of mind" (IX, 1122-5). After they have repented, and Raphael tells Adam of the coming of the Messiah, Adam acknowledges the Messiah as his redeemer (XII, 572). Although he and Eve have to leave paradise, they have attained a kind of paradise within themselves (XII, 585-7).

The final resolution of the poem reveals that the entire epic is a preparation for the coming of the Messiah. The Messiah unites Adam and Eve with God by fulfilling their duty to obey God. He pays the ransom for their sins and redeems them from death. He defeats Sin and Death, and he ascends to heaven in victory.

Milton's attitude toward Eve is that she is inferior to Adam in intellect and temperament. Adam is created in the image of God, i.e. he reflects God's image, but Eve is created from Adam and therefore only secondarily reflects God's image. She represents the weaker, less astute and less prudent side of Adam's character. She says to Adam, "My Author and Disposer, what thou bidd'st/Unargu'd I obey; so God ordains,/God is thy law, thou mine: to know no more/Is woman's happiest knowledge and her praise" (IV, 635-8). According to Milton, it is a wife's duty to obey her husband. The downfall of Adam and Eve is caused by her failure to heed his warning that they should remain together in order to guard against any malicious spirit that may be hovering nearby. Adam says, "The Wife, where danger or dishonor lurks,/Safest and seemliest by her

Husband stays" (IX, 267-8). This misogynistic attitude on Milton's part is an unfortunate aspect of the poem.

Recurrent images in *Paradise Lost* include the fruit and the garden, light and darkness, ethereal vapors and pestilent fumes, blazing swords and flaming chariots, winged heralds and celestial armies, royal sceptres and imperial thrones.

Milton suggests that knowledge is not intrinsically good and that in order for it to be good it must be combined with wisdom. Knowledge can be fatal if it is used unwisely: "One fatal Tree there stands of Knowledge call'd" (IV, 514). Thus, Adam's and Eve's tasting of the fruit of the tree of knowledge leads to their expulsion from the garden of Eden.

Milton's attitude toward Satan's rebellion against God is consistent with his political writings on the powers and duties of the English monarchy. In his treatise entitled "The Tenure of Kings and Magistrates" (1649), Milton says that human beings are naturally born free, but that in order to promote their well-being and security they must unite under a sovereign who can protect and defend them against aggression. Kings only have as much authority as is given to them by their subjects. The authority of kings over their subjects is based on their promoting the well-being and security of their subjects, and it is also based on their acting in accordance with principles of justice. To say that kings are not accountable to their subjects is therefore to overturn the principles of justice and civil government.

In Milton's *Paradise Lost,* Satan's rebellion against God is not a struggle against injustice, but a selfish attempt to attain prestige and power. Satan's persuasion of the fallen angels to accept him as their commander is a devious and cynical attempt to overthrow a rightful monarchy. God rules the universe with love, wisdom, and justice, but Satan wants to rule the universe by means of subterfuge, coercion, and intimidation. God has created Adam and Eve free to act according to reason, but Satan wants to enslave them. God's kingdom is a realm of light, but Satan's kingdom is a realm of darkenss.

Artists who have produced illustrations for editions of *Paradise Lost* include John Baptist de Medina (1688), Francis Hayman (1749), James Barry (1792, etchings and engravings), Henry Fuseli (1802, illustrations based on paintings), William Blake (1806), John Martin (1827, etchings), Gustave Doré (1866, engravings), William Hyde (1904, etchings and engravings), and Mary Groom (1937, engravings).

The Symbolization of Evil

Satan as a symbol of evil, temptation, malevolence, and hatred has undergone many historical transformations. He has been variously called the devil (*el diablo, le diable, der Teufel*, etc.), Lucifer, the Prince of Darkness, Beelzebub, and Mephistopheles. The degree to which he is perceived as an actual being or merely as a symbol has changed historically and may vary from culture to culture.

Mephistopheles is a character in the sixteenth century *Faustbuch* (a German folk book that was first printed in 1587) and in Christopher Marlowe's play *The Tragical History of Doctor Faustus* (1588, as "Mephistophilis"). Mephistopheles is also a character in Johann Wolfgang von Goethe's dramatic poem, *Faust* (Part 1, 1808, Part 2, 1832), which inspired Robert Schumann's *Scenes from Goethe's Faust* (1844-53), Franz Liszt's *A Faust Symphony* (1857), and Charles Gounod's opera *Faust* (1859). The Faust legend of a scholar who sells his soul to the devil in exchange for knowledge also inspired Hector Berlioz' opera, *La Damnation de Faust* (*The Damnation of Faust*, 1893).

Many characters in literature and film have in one way or another been icons of evil or likenesses of Satan (e.g. Iago, Vautrin, Dorian Gray, Uriah Heep, Kurz, Ahab, Magua, Mr. Hyde, Professor Moriarty, Captain Bligh, The Wicked Witch of the West, Hannibal Lecter, Dr. No, Auric Goldfinger, Max Cady, Freddy Krueger, Lex Luthor, and Darth Vader). An interesting example is Dracula, who loses his power if he is in the presence of sacred symbols such as a crucifix, a holy wafer, or holy water.

The Controversy Concerning Literal vs. Symbolic Interpretation of Scripture

The question of whether the story of Adam and Eve should be interpreted as a myth or as an account of actual historical events is controversial. This question also leads to another question, whether everything in the Bible should be interpreted literally or whether some passages should be interpreted as symbolic expressions of divine revelation. Other stories in the Bible (e.g. the story of Noah and the Ark, the story of Jonah and the Whale) may also be interpreted as myths (or may be interpreted as actual historical events, depending on one's point of view), but to interpret them as myths is not necessarily to say that they are lacking in truth or meaning. To insist that everything in the Bible must be interpreted literally may actually be to attempt to deprive God's revelation of its mystery and depth of meaning. Interpretation of the stories of Jonah and the Whale or of

Adam and Eve as myths may enable us to attain a deeper understanding of their true symbolic power. Thus, it may be as wrong to attempt to demythologize the Bible as to insist that everything in the Bible must be interpreted literally.

Rudolf Bultmann (1953) argues that the cosmology of the New Testament is essentially mythical in character and that it views the world as a three-level structure with the earth in the center, heaven above, and the underworld below.[4] He claims that this mythic view of the world is obsolete and that there is nothing in it that is intrinsically Christian. It is simply a mode of pre-scientific thinking. Blind acceptance of this mythology would be irrational, and to insist on its acceptance as an article of faith would be to accept a view of the world in our religion and faith which we would not accept in everyday life.[5]

Bultmann's viewpoint is controversial, but Helmut Thielicke (1953) explains that Bultmann is trying to liberate the New Testament from mythology and to interpret it in the context of the modern world. For Bultmann, the mythological aspect of the New Testament affects its message, and this mythological aspect is not an intrinsic part of the message. Thus, the mythic aspect of the New Testament must be reinterpeted from a more modern viewpoint. However, Thielicke also notes that this reinterpretation does not consider the resurrection to be the source of our faith but instead considers our faith to be the source of the resurrection. Thus, the resurrection becomes merely a symbol, and Bultmann's viewpoint fails to recognize the resurrection as an event in its own right.

Christian mythological figures include Santa Claus (Saint Nicholas), Saint George (slayer of the dragon), Samson (who, according to Judges 14:6, killed a lion with his bare hands), and the knights of the Grail legend (Sir Perceval and Sir Galahad).

Myths and their Symbolic Function

Claude Lévi-Strauss (1963) explains that myths may serve as explanations for phenomena that we cannot otherwise understand. Through myths, we can reconstruct events such as the origin of the universe or the beginnings of humankind. Myths are timeless, because they explain the present and the past as well as the future.[6]

---

4. Rudolf Bultmann, "New Testament and Mythology," in *Kerygma and Myth: A Theological Debate*, edited by Hans Werner Bartsch, translated by Reginald H. Fuller (London: S.P.C.K., 1953), p. 1.
5. *Ibid.*, p. 4.

According to Lévi-Strauss, the meaning of a myth may depend on the way in which its structural elements are combined. Since myths are a mode of language, their constituent elements (mythemes) presuppose and are structurally more complex than the basic elements of language (phonemes, morphemes, sememes, etc.). Mythemes are not isolated relations, but complexes of relations that may evolve over a period of time. Relations between mythemes may be synchronic (horizontal) or diachronic (vertical). Structural analysis of myths or mythemes must therefore be both synchronic and diachronic, and diachronic analysis must consider all the variants of a given myth or mytheme that have occurred over a period of time.

Myths are tales or traditional stories that attempt to express basic truths about the nature of human society and about the nature of the physical world. *Mythos* is a Greek term for tale or story, as distinguished from *logos* (reason or law), *pathos* (an emotional appeal), and *ethos* (an appeal based on the character of the speaker) as a method of persuasion or explanation.

Joseph Campbell (1949) describes the tale of the mythological hero as a "monomyth" from which many other myths are derived. The heroic cycle of separation, initiation, and return is the nuclear unit of the monomyth, which corresponds to a rite of passage. The mythological hero sets forth from the ordinary world, and he reaches a world of supernatural wonder, where he confronts threatening forces and wins a decisive victory. He then returns to the ordinary world, with the power to bestow benefits on humankind. The cycle includes a call to adventure, which leads to the crossing of a theshold and to a brother-battle, a dragon-battle, an abduction, a night-sea journey, a journey in a whale's belly, or a wonder journey. The hero may be given aid by magical helpers. At the nadir of the cycle, the hero undergoes a supreme ordeal and may descend into the realm of death, but he rises again and gains victory. His triumph may be represented by a sacred marriage, an apotheosis, or the taking of a prize. The hero's return to the world may then be a reemergence from the kingdom of dread.

Paul Ricoeur (1967) explains that one of the symbolic functions of myths is to reveal the bond between human beings and the sacred. Myths are "hierophanies,"[7] i.e. revelations of the sacred. Demythologization is a mode of modern thought in which the pseudo-knowledge or false *logos* of myth from a scientific

---

6. Claude Lévi-Strauss, *Structural Anthropology*, translated by Claire Jacobson and Brooke Schoepf (New York: Basic Books, 1963), p. 109.
7. This term was coined by Mircea Eliade, in *The Sacred and the Profane*, translated by Willard R. Trask (New York: Harcourt, Brace, and Co., 1959).

standpoint is abandoned, so that myth can be rediscovered as myth. Thus, Ricoeur distinguishes between "demythologizing" and "demythicizing."[8]

The dynamics of mythical symbols, according to Ricoeur, consist in the fact that every symbol is iconoclastic in relation to some other symbol, just as every symbol, if seen in isolation, tends to be solidified by idolatry. The stability or instability of mythical symbols must therefore be recognized by a hermeneutics that actively participates in these dynamics.[9]

Dante's *Divine Comedy*

Another notable example of Christian semiotics in epic poetry is Dante's *Divine Comedy* (1308-1321). Widely regarded as one of the greatest poems in Western literature, it presents an awe-inspiring vision of hell, purgatory, and paradise. From its harrowing and morbidly fascinating depiction of the tortures of hell to its mystical and transcendently beautiful description of the planets of paradise, the *Divine Comedy* tells a story of profound religious and moral significance.

Dante Alighieri (1265-1321) was an Italian poet who was born in Florence. His father, Alighirro di Bellincione di Alighiero, was a notary or lawyer. His mother, Donna Bella, died sometime between 1270 and 1273 when Dante was still a boy. His father remarried and had one son and two daughters by his second marriage, but he died sometime before 1283. At the age of nine, Dante met a girl named Bice Portinari (c.1265-1290), the daughter of a neighbor. She was eight years old when they first met. He called her Beatrice, and although they did not meet again until nine years later, he developed a lifelong emotional attachment to her. There is no evidence that she reciprocated his feelings. She was married to a wealthy banker named Simone de' Bardi in about 1287, and she died in 1290. Dante was married sometime before 1292 to Gemma Donati. He and Gemma had been betrothed to each other at an early age as part of an arranged marriage. They had at least three children, Jacopo, Pietro, and Antonia. From 1293 onward, Dante was involved in the political conflict between the Guelf and Ghibelline factions in Florence. Allying himself with the "White Guelfs" who favored independence from the influence of the pope and the Holy Roman Emperor, he took part in the military victory at Campaldino, in which Florence defeated the Ghibellines. As a magistrate of Florence, he was responsible for the exile of his

---

8. Paul Ricoeur, *The Symbolism of Evil*, translated by Emerson Buchanan (Boston: Beacon Press, 1967), p. 352.
9. *Ibid.*, p. 354.

wife's cousin, Corso di Donati, who was a leader of the "Black Guelfs," and he also banished his best friend, the poet Guido Cavalcanti (1230-1300), who was a prominent White Guelf. Dante was sent on a diplomatic mission to the court of Pope Boniface VIII in Rome in 1301, but when the Black Guelfs returned to power later that year, he was forced into exile. Living a wandering life for a number of years, he finally settled in Ravenna in 1318. During his exile, he was not accompanied by his wife, but his sons Jacopo and Pietro and his daughter Antonia joined him in Ravenna. Antonia entered a convent in Ravenna, and she took the name "Sister Beatrice." Dante became ill while on a diplomatic mission to Venice in 1321, and he returned to Ravenna, where he died. His masterpiece, *La Commedia di Dante Alighieri* (*The Comedy of Dante Alighieri*) was begun in about 1308 and for the most part completed by 1315. The last section was completed shortly before his death. The poem was not given the title, "Divine Comedy," until two centuries later. Dante's other major works include *La Vita Nuova* (c. 1292, *The New Life*), which is an autobiographical collection of sonnets, lyrics, and prose.

The *Commedia* is divided into three canticles: *L'Inferno* (*Hell*), *Il Purgatorio* (*Purgatory*), and *Il Paradiso* (*Paradise*). Each canticle contains 33 cantos, with an additional introductory canto in *L'Inferno*, making a total of 100 cantos. Each canto contains approximately 130-150 stanzas, written in terza rima (three-line stanzas, interlinked by a regular rhyme scheme with the second line of each stanza rhyming with the first and third of the next).

The main characters in the poem are Dante, Vergil, and Beatrice. Dante is guided through hell and purgatory by the poet Vergil, who then turns him over to Beatrice, an angelic figure who guides him through paradise.

The story begins on Maundy Thursday evening in the year 1300. Dante is lost in a dark forest. He tries to make his way along a hillside, but his path is blocked by a leopard, then by a lion, then by a wolf. As he returns to the forest, he meets the shadow of Virgil, who offers to guide him by a longer way leading through hell and purgatory, the first two of the three realms that Dante must visit. Dante accepts Virgil as his master and guide, and they begin the journey. (canto I).

They arrive at the gates of hell on Good Friday evening (canto III), and they enter the vestibule. Coming to the river Acheron, they are ferried across by Charon, and they reach the edge of the pit of hell. They enter the first circle (Limbo), where they meet the souls of unbaptized and virtuous pagans, Homer, Horace, Electra, Hector, Aeneas, Socrates, Plato, Thales, Zeno, Empedocles, Euclid, Ptolemy, and others. They then proceed to the second circle (the realm of the lustful), where they meet Cleopatra, Helen, Paris, Achilles, and Dante also speaks to Francesca da Rimini (canto V).

In the third circle, Cerberus, the three-headed dog of the underworld, clutches and rips apart the souls of the gluttonous. Dante and Vergil continue through the fourth and fifth circles of hell to the river Styx (Holy Saturday morning), and they are ferried across the Styx to the city of Dis (canto VIII). At the city walls, they happen to meet the father of Guido Cavalcanti, and Dante tells him of Guido's death. A heavenly messenger opens the gates of Dis, and Virgil and Dante enter the city. They come to the river Phlegethon, a river of boiling blood in which those who have been violent against their neighbors (Attila, Alexander the Great, and others) are boiling. The banks of the river are guarded by centaurs, and Virgil asks the centaur Chiron to send Nessus to carry Dante across the river (canto XII).

Reaching a steep precipice, the poets climb onto the back of the monster Geryon and are carried over the barrier to the eighth circle (canto XVII). Dante talks to the flatterers who wallow in excrement. The panderers and seducers are being beaten with whips, the simoniacs (those who have sold ecclesiastical preferments) are being tortured by flames that lick at their feet, and the walls of the pit are covered with slime. After proceeding further, Dante and Virgil reach the well at the bottom of the abyss, around which stand the giants who are visible from the waist up. The poets see Nimrod and Ephialtes, and they are lowered over the edge of the pit by the giant Antaeus (canto XXXI). In the ninth circle, they come to the frozen lake of Cocytus, in which the souls of traitors are permanetly immersed. Dis (Satan) is standing in the center of the lake. He has three faces, and he is devouring Judas, Brutus, and Cassius in each of his three mouths (end of Part I).

On Easter Sunday morning, Dante and Virgil emerge from hell, and they meet Cato, the guardian of the mountain of purgatory. Cato instructs Virgil to wash the filth of hell from Dante's face and to gird his waist with reeds from the island before they begin their ascent. They climb to the first terrace and meet Manfred, the son of the Emperor Frederick II (canto III). They proceed to the second terrace, where they meet Sordello, a troubadour who leads them to a beautiful valley. A serpent enters the valley but is chased away by two angels (canto VIII). Dante falls asleep and has a dream in which he is lifted up by an eagle. He awakens on Easter Monday morning to find that during the night he has been carried away by Saint Lucy and has been taken to the gate of purgatory. He and Virgil meet a porter who invites Dante to climb the three steps leading to the gate, which represent the three parts of penitence: confession, contrition, and satisfaction.[10] The porter then inscribes Dante's forehead with seven P's (standing for *peccatum* or "sin"; each P stands for one of the seven deadly sins), and he opens the gate with the keys of Saint Peter (canto IX).

As the poets climb each cornice, the marks of the seven deadly sins are successively erased from Dante's forehead. At the first cornice (representing pride), the angel of humility erases the first P. At the second cornice (representing envy), the angel of generosity erases the second P. At the third cornice (representing anger), the angel of meekness erases the third P. At the fourth cornice (representing sloth), the angel of zeal erases the fourth P.

On Tuesday morning, the poets reach the fifth cornice (representing covetousness), where they meet Statius, a fellow-poet and admirer of Virgil, who leads them to the pass between the the fifth and sixth cornices. The angel of liberality erases the fifth P from Dante's forehead. At the sixth cornice (representing gluttony), they meet Dante's friend, Forese Donati, who tells them about the other souls in purgatory. The angel of temperance erases the sixth P, and they ascend through the pass to the seventh cornice. At the seventh cornice (representing lust), the angel of chastity erases the seventh P from Dante's forehead.

On Wednesday morning, Virgil leaves Dante as they ascend from the seventh cornice, and Dante finds himself in earthly paradise. He enters a sacred wood, where he meets Matilda, a "fair lady" who is singing and gathering flowers. Beatrice arrives in a chariot (end of Part II), and they ascend to the planet Mercury, where Dante meets his friend Charles Martel. They continue to ascend to Venus and to the heaven of the sun, where they are surrounded by twelve lights. St. Thomas Aquinas identifies himself as one of the twelve, the others being Albertus Magnus, Gratian, Peter Lombard, Solomon, Dionysius the Areopagite, Orosius, Boethius, Isidore of Seville, Bede, Richard of St. Victor, and Sigier of Brabant. The circle of lights is then surrounded by another circle of twelve lights, which includes St. Bonaventure, Illuminato, Fra Agostino, Hugh of St. Victor, Petrus Comestor, Peter of Spain, Nathan, St. Chrysostom, St. Anselm, Donatus, Rabanus, and Joachim of Flora.[11] The double circle of lights tells Dante and Beatrice of the mystery of the Holy Trinity.

Dante finds himself in the heaven of Mars, and he has a vision of Christ. He then meets his great-great-grandfather, who tells him about twelfth-century Flo-

---

10. Dorothy L. Sayers, *The Comedy of Dante Alighieri, the Florentine. Cantica II: Purgatory (Il Purgatorio)*, (Harmondsworth: Penguin Books, 1955), p. 139.
11. Barbara Reynolds, *The Comedy of Dante Alighieri, the Florentine, Cantica III: Paradise (Il Paradiso)*, translated by Dorothy L. Sayers and Barbara Reynolds (Harmondsworth: Penguin Books, 1962), p. 166.

rence. Dante ascends with Beatrice to the heaven of Jupiter, where the spirits of the just transform themselves into a symbol of justice, the eagle. David is the light of the eye of the eagle, and the lights above the eye are formed by Trajan, Hezekiah, Constantine, William II of Sicily, and Rhipeus the Trojan.

Dante and Beatrice ascend to Saturn, where they meet Peter Damian and St. Benedict. Dante beholds the light of Christ and the lights of the Virgin Mary and the apostles (canto XXVIII). He talks with Saints Peter, James, and John. Finally, he ascends with Beatrice to the primum mobile and to the empyrean, where St. Bernard invites Dante to gaze upon the celestial rose. St. Bernard prays to the Virgin Mary that Dante may be granted grace and purity of heart, and after Mary gazes upward into the eternal light, Dante also gazes upward and has a vision of God.

The cosmology of the poem is quite intricate, with multiple descending levels of sinfulness in hell, multiple ascending levels of penitence on Mount Purgatory, and multiple ascending levels of divine grace in heavenly paradise. Hell is conceived as a funnel-shaped pit which extends from the northern hemisphere to the center of the earth. Mount Purgatory is situated on an island in the southern hemisphere, and above it is the earthly paradise. There are nine circles of hell, nine levels of purgatory (two terraces and seven cornices), and nine heavens, with the empyrean as an even higher heaven.

In Dante's hell, the least sinful souls are in the upper levels of the pit, and the most sinful souls are in the lower levels of the pit, with Satan at the very bottom. Incontinent souls are condemned to the second through fifth circles, violent souls are condemned to the seventh circle, and fraudulent souls are condemned to the eighth and ninth circles. The vestibule of hell is reserved for those who have not committed themselves to Christ. Limbo, the first circle, is reserved for unbaptized virtuous pagans, i.e. those who have not had the opportunity to commit themselves to Christ.[12] In the second circle of hell are the lustful, in the third circle the gluttonous, in the fourth circle the prodigal and the avaricious, in the fifth circle the wrathful, in the sixth circle the heretics, in the seventh circle the violent (against neighbors, against themselves, and against God), in the eighth circle the fraudulent (including panderers, seducers, flatterers, simoniacs, fortune tellers, grafters, hypocrites, thieves, fraudulent counselors, sowers of discord, and falsifiers), and in the ninth circle the traitors and the treacherously fraudulent (to kin, to homeland, to guests, and to benefactors).

---

12. Dorothy L. Sayers, *The Comedy of Dante Alighieri, the Florentine, Cantica I: Hell (L'Inferno)*, (Harmondsworth: Penguin Books, 1949), p. 95.

Mount Purgatory is a place where those who have repented can expiate their sins. It has two terraces at the bottom, leading upward to Peter's gate, and then seven progressively higher cornices. The first terrace is reserved for excommunicants, and the second for those who are too late in repenting of their sins. On the first cornice are those who are proud, on the second those who are envious, on the third those who are wrathful, on the fourth those who are slothful, on the fifth those who are covetous, on the sixth those who are gluttonous, and on the seventh those who are lustful.

The system of penance that is enacted on Mount Purgatory is very harsh and demanding. The penance of the proud consists of having to bow down below the weight of heavy stones (canto X). The penance of the envious consists of having their eyes sealed shut (canto XIII). The penance of the wrathful consists of having to make their way through a cloud of black smoke (canto XVI). The penance of the slothful consists of having to run uphill (canto XVIII). The penance of the covetous requires them to lay face-down on the ground (canto XIX). The penance of the gluttonous consists of having to endure starvation (canto XX). And the penance of the lustful consists of having to endure flaming heat (canto XXV).

Above Mount Purgatory in Dante's universe, earthly paradise is a realm from which those who have attained grace can ascend to heavenly paradise. In the heavens are first the moon, then Mercury, then Venus, then the Sun, then Mars, then Jupiter, then Saturn, then the fixed stars, then the primum mobile (the "first mover" which directs the movements of the other heavens), and then the empyrean (the highest heaven).

For Dante, faith, hope, and love are the three celestial virtues (canto VII, *Paradise*). Those who do not repent of their sins are doomed to hell. Those who have repented of their sins can expiate them in purgatory and can be absolved. Penitence includes confession, contrition, and, reparation or making amends for one's misdeeds. Absolution is possible for anyone who repents and who does sufficient penitence, but faith, hope, and love are also required for entry into paradise.

Virgil tells Dante in Canto XVIII of *Purgatory* that human beings have the power of free will. Human beings are capable of mastering their own appetites and passions. Thus, Virgil is able to resign his guardianship of Dante after they have ascended Mount Purgatory, because Dante has attained mastery over himself. Beatrice also tells Dante in paradise (canto V) that free will is God's greatest gift to human beings and that it is the human quality which most resembles the freedom of God. Thus, if we vow to surrender our own self-will and to accept God's will, we are making a sacred vow, and we cannot atone for failing to keep such a vow by merely doing good works.

A central theme of the *Divine Comedy* is that there is a system of divine justice that ultimately punishes those who are sinful and that ultimately rewards those who are righteous. This system of justice is absolute and unequivocal. There is no remission of punishment for sin until repentance has occurred and until penitence has been fully performed. Salvation requires faith, hope, and love, which are personified in the poem by Beatrice. She is a beatific figure for Dante; she bestows blessedness upon the poet and leads him to God. She also symbolizes the revelation of divine justice. Through her intervention, he is able to overcome his doubts about divine justice and is able to recognize the truth of faith.

In the poem, Virgil represents divine grace. He is a source of wisdom, friendship, and spiritual guidance for Dante. He is described as kind, courteous, steadfast, and as having a noble soul. Dante acknowledges him as "master," and he also addresses him as "my lord." Virgil is a stabilizing influence on Dante's emotions during the journey through hell. He constantly reassures Dante that paradise is ahead. He occasionally warns him not to linger at various points along the way, and he gives him permission to speak to the souls whom they meet in hell and purgatory. Dante addresses him as "father," and Virgil addresses Dante as "son" (*Purgatory*, canto IV). Virgil carries Dante in his arms as they descend through the eighth circle of hell. However, Virgil is not able to enter heaven, because of his own lack of faith (*Purgatory*, canto VII). He tells Dante that a worthier spirit must guide him from purgatory to the realm of heavenly bliss.

Virgil's washing of Dante's face after they have reached the island of purgatory is a symbolic baptism, preparing Dante for his journey up the mountain. Dante says that he has been washed clean of the disfiguring smears of hell (*Purgatory*, I, 129).

A recurrent image in the poem is Dante's shadow, reminding him of the materiality of his own body and of the immateriality of the souls who dwell in hell and purgatory. The shades of the dead cast no shadow, so Dante's shadow alerts the shades that a living being has entered their midst. His shadow also symbolizes his mortality, since it appears as the sun is setting.

It should be noted that Dante's depiction of the prophet Muhammad as a soul in the inferno (canto XXVIII) is based on the medieval Christian view of the Prophet as a sower of discord. This view obviously belongs to the past and is incompatible with a modern Christian world-view, which must recognize the importance of mutual toleration among people of all religions. Modern Christianity teaches the importance of respect for all religious faiths. Dante's message in canto XXVIII of *The Inferno* should be condemned, and his language and use of imagery in this canto are offensive. It should also be noted, however, that he consigns several popes (Nicholas III, Boniface VIII, and Clement V) to the inferno, accusing them of being greedy and avaricious (canto XIX).

The Divine Comedy describes a spiritual journey that is universal in its meaning. According to Dante, the life of the human spirit is a passage through ascending levels of awareness and revelation of the wisdom, truth, and justice of God. Salvation requires self-examination, insight into one's faults, confession of one's misdeeds, repentance, and penitence, all of which depend upon divine grace. Divine grace is universally offered to all believers, and paradise awaits all who complete the journey.

In what sense is the poem a comedy? It is comedic in the sense that all of the souls in hell and purgatory, including Virgil and Dante, have shortcomings and failings from which we can learn. Their shortcomings can enlighten and inform us about the weaknesses of human nature and can serve as examples of human error and imperfection. The weaknesses of human nature are described in meticulous detail, and at several points in the narrative, Dante is overcome by the revelation of the torments suffered by those who have sinned, and he falls into a swoon.

Other recurrent images in the poem include Dante's dreams while he is sleeping, which may signify temporary illusion and his awakening to reality, and the choirs of angels that sing in the heavenly paradise, which may symbolize divine revelation and the zeal of righteousness.

The symbolism of the number three in the poem is a reference to the Trinity and to the triadic nature of cosmic order. The poem is divided into three canticles, each having 33 cantos, each canto divided into three-line stanzas. The universe is divided into three realms: hell, purgatory, and paradise. Hell is divided into three divisions (circles two through five for the incontinent, circle seven for the violent, and circles eight and nine for the fraudulent). Virgil, Dante, and Beatrice represent three stages of faith. At the beginning of the poem, Dante is confronted by three beasts, representing the three cardinal sins (lust, pride, and avarice). During his journey through hell, he falls asleep three times. In the bottom of the pit of hell, Satan has three faces and three mouths. Purgatory is divided into three stages: lower, middle, and upper, corresponding to perverted love, defective love, and excessive love. When Dante meets his friend Casella in purgatory, he momentarily forgets that Casella is only a shadow, and he attempts to embrace him three times. Three steps lead to Peter's gate. There are three realms of paradise: an earthly paradise, a heavenly paradise, and an empyrean. There are three celestial virtues: faith, hope, and love. Three ladies in the poem help Dante to complete his journey: Beatrice, Saint Lucy, and the Virgin Mary.

The number symbolism of the poem also includes various multiples of the number three. There are nine circles of hell, nine levels of purgatory (two terraces and seven cornices), and nine heavens. When Dante and Beatrice reach the heaven of the sun, they are surrounded by a circle of twelve lights, which revolve around them three times. Then they are surrounded by a second circle of twelve lights and by a third circle of light (*Paradise*, canto XIV). In the heaven of Jupiter, they see an eagle whose eye and eyebrow are composed of six lights (canto XX). In the primum mobile, Dante sees nine circles of light reflected in Beatrice's eyes, which represent the nine angelic orders (cherubim, seraphim, thrones, dominions, authorities, powers, principalities, archangels, and angels, canto XXVIII).

The image of an eagle also appears at three important stages of the poem. When Dante falls asleep in purgatory after climbing the second terrace, he dreams of being carried away by an eagle. In his dream, the eagle carries him into a sphere of flame, symbolically purifying his soul. When Beatrice meets him in the earthly paradise, she is riding in a chariot drawn by a griffin (a creature with the head and wings of an eagle and the body of a lion). And when Dante and Beatrice reach the heaven of Jupiter, the spirits form the shape of an eagle, symbolizing justice.

The Christian Imagination

Many other examples of the creativity and power of the Christian imagination can be found in the semiotics of art and literature. The study of Christian semiotics can help us to better understand the influence of the aesthetic or literary imagination on Christian theology and the influence of Christian theology on the aesthetic or literary imagination.

The Christian imagination is theological, moral, poetic, and philosophical. It is appraisive, valuative, prescriptive, and formative. It may transcend any classification or categorization.

According to Janine Langan (2002), the Christian imagination is anti-Gnostic, because it views reality as a mode of revelation and because it regards the world as an unfolding mystery in which we can all participate.[13] It is typological, because it views life as a meaningful history whose structure is revealed by Christ.

---

13. The Gnostics of the early centuries C.E. believed that all physical matter is evil and that the world was created by an evil demiurge. They denied that Jesus had a corporeal existence. They believed that they alone held the *gnosis* or secret knowledge which is the key to salvation.

It is iconic, because it attempts to reflect the face of God. It is sacramental, because it aims to participate in the reality of God's presence and because it also aims to recognize signs of God's presence throughout the universe. And it is eschatological, because it is attuned to the paradoxical nature of creation.[14]

---

14. Janine Langan, "The Christian Imagination," in *The Christian Imagination*, edited by Leland Ryken (Colorado Springs: Shaw Books, 2002), pp.63-80.

Chapter VI

CHRISTIAN ETHICS

The Scope of its Concerns

Christian ethics may be another field of study for Christian semiotics. There may be many ways to define "Christian ethics" or "Christian values," and Christians may take many different approaches to ethical decision making. The assumption that there is a definable set of "Christian values" may be based on the fact that there are some principles of conduct, such as the Ten Commandments,[1] that Christians generally regard as moral imperatives. There may also be other standards of conduct, such as altruism, compassion, forgiveness, generosity, fairness, and tolerance that are generally agreed to be Christian ideals or values. However, there may be many different interpretations of how to apply these ideals or values to situations in everyday life.

It should be noted that the term "Christian values" has been used in political discourse to denote a particular set of attitudes regarding such issues as abortion, contraception, the role of the family as a social unit, and prayer in public schools. The term, however, may be used more broadly to include such principles as faith, love, kindness, fellowship, righteousness, and justice.

Christian ethics may be divided into three main areas: 1) metaethics, which studies the nature of ethical decision making, 2) normative ethics, which prescribes codes of conduct, and 3) applied ethics, which studies the application of ethical principles to everyday life. Of these three main areas, the greatest controversy tends to occur in the area of applied ethics, which includes such fields as biomedical ethics (regarding genetic engineering, embryonic stem cell research, in-vitro fertilization, cloning, contraception, abortion, euthanasia etc.), professional ethics, business ethics, military ethics, human rights, animal rights, environmental ethics, and the ethics of capital punishment. There may be many different interpretations of how to apply the teachings of Christianity to these areas of decision making.

Metaethics considers questions such as, "How do we determine what is morally right or wrong?" and "Is it always possible for us to know what is morally right or wrong?" Normative ethics considers questions such as, "What should be the goal of ethical conduct?" and "What is the best way to promote our own well-being and the well-being of society?"

In metaethics, there may be considerable variation among Christians as to the importance attached to official Church doctrine and to the teachings of the

---

1. 1) Do not worship false gods, 2) do not worship graven images, 3) do not misuse the name of God, 4) keep the sabbath holy, 5) honor your father and mother, 6) do not kill, 7) do not commit adultery, 8) do not steal, 9) do not lie, 10) do not covet.

Church. Some Christians may rely more on the teachings of the Church than others in making decisions about ethical issues.

Christians may also have varying opinons about such questions as whether moral truth is determined by faith or by reason, whether propositions contradictory to reason can be verified by divine revelation, and whether there are moral facts or only moral interpretations of facts

In normative ethics, Christians may also have varying opinions about such questions as whether there are moral absolutes with regard to standards of conduct, whether there is an acceptable rate of civilian casualties during the waging of a war, and whether infringements of the rights of some individuals can be justified by a supposed benefit to society as a whole.

Metaethical Theories

Approaches to metaethics include ideal judgment theory, ideal moral agent theory, divine command theory, ethical naturalism, ethical relativism, cognitivism, and noncognitivism.

Ideal judgment theory affirms that the rightness or wrongness of moral judgments is determined by whether they would be the judgments of an ideal judge under ideal conditions.

Ideal moral agent theory affirms that the rightness or wrongness of an action is determined by whether the action is the one that would be chosen under the same conditions by an ideal moral agent.

Divine command theory (also called theological voluntarism) affirms that the rightness or wrongness of an action is determined by whether the action is commanded or willed by God.

Ethical naturalism affirms that natural laws govern the rightness or wrongness of human judgments and actions.

Ethical relativism asserts that the rightness or wrongness of actions depends on their context. Actions that are wrong in one context may be right in another context, and vice versa.

Cognitivism asserts that ethical judgments have a propositional content and that they can therefore be described as true or false. Non-cognitvism asserts that ethical judgments are not propositions, but rather expressions of emotions, feelings, or attitudes which cannot be described as true or false. Non-cognitivist theories include emotivism (the theory that ethical judgments are expressions of emotions), prescriptivism (the theory that ethical judgments are commands or prescriptions and not declarative utterances), and expressivism (the theory that ethical judgments are speech-acts that express our approval or disapproval of various actions).

All of the above approaches to metaethics are compatible with Christian ethics. However, two other approaches, skepticism and nihilism, are incompatible with Christian ethics. Skepticism suspends judgment about the rightness or wrongness of all ethical judgments, and nihilism asserts that all ethical judgments are meaningless and that there are no objective criteria for determining whether any action is right or wrong. In contrast, Christian ethics affirm that there are objective principles of moral conduct by which we can decide whether our actions are right or wrong. Christian ethics also affirm that our moral choices are always meaningful and that they have personal or social consequences.

Normative Ethical Theories

Approaches to normative ethics include deontology, consequentialism, intuitionism, and virtue ethics.

Deontological or formalistic ethics assert that the rightness or wrongness of actions is determined by whether they conform to formal principles of duty or to rules of conduct. Thus, the rightness or wrongness of actions is determined by their motives and not by their consequences.

Kantian ethics are an example of deontological ethics. According to Immanuel Kant (1785), the moral value of an action is determined by whether the action is motivated by a sense of duty. Actions which conform to duty but which are not motivated by a sense of duty have less moral value than those which both conform to duty and are motivated by duty. If an action is motivated by duty, then the moral value of the action is determined not by the purpose for which the action is performed, but by the principle according to which the action is decided upon. Thus, the moral value of an action is determined not by how effective the action is in achieving its aim, but by the principle of volition according to which the action is performed.[2]

Kant says that the "categorical imperative" is to act in such a way that the principle according to which an action is performed may be accepted as a universal law of morality. The categorical imperative is therefore a duty to "act only in such a way that you can will that the maxim of your action should become a universal law."[3] This moral imperative is also a duty to act according to an objective

---

2. Immanuel Kant, *Groundwork of the Metaphysic of Morals*, translated by H.J. Paton (New York: Harper & Row, 1964), p. 68.

principle of reason. Since the human will may not always be completely determined by reason, Kant emphasizes that subjective principles of volition should conform to objective principles of reason. The categorical imperative is necessary only for an imperfect will. A perfect will aims to do everything that is logically necessary and has no need of any moral imperatives, because it seeks to do only what is good.

Kant also says that moral imperatives may be hypothetical or categorical. A hypothetical imperative determines an action to be practically necessary for the achievment of some purpose beyond the action itself. On the other hand, a categorical imperative determines an action to objectively necessary, regardless of any purpose beyond the action itself. If the purpose of an action is abandoned, then a hypothetical imperative may determine that the action is no longer necessary, but a categorical imperative determines the action to be necessary under all conditions, and it affirms that the action is good in itself.

In contrast to deontological ethics, which assert that the rightness or wrongness of an action is determined by its motives and by whether it conforms to moral duty, teleological or consequentialist ethics assert that the rightness or wrongness of an action is determined only by its consequences. Utilitarianism and pragmatism are examples of teleological ethics.

Utilitarianism, as defined by J.S. Mill (1863), is a theory that the rightness or wrongness of actions is determined by whether they conform to the principle of utility (the greatest happiness principle), i.e. by whether they promote happiness or prevent unhappiness for the greatest possible number of individuals. Actions are morally right insofar as they tend to promote happiness or prevent unhappiness. Actions are morally wrong insofar as they tend to prevent happiness or promote unhappiness.

According to Mill, the utility of an action may be determiend not merely by the amount of happiness which the action produces for the individual who performs the action, but by the total amount of happiness which the action produces for all individuals. Thus, the utility of an action may be determined by the total amount of happiness which may be enjoyed, or by the total amount of unhappiness which may be suffered, by all individuals who are affected by the action.

Mill affirms that it is morally right for an individual to sacrifice some degree of personal happiness if this act of sacrifice increases the total amount of happiness that may be enjoyed by all individuals. However, he denies that the act of self-sacrifice is intrinsically good, and he says that the act of self-sacrifice is bad if it

---

3. *Ibid.*, p. 70.

produces a lesser total amount of happiness for all individuals or a greater total amount of unhappiness for all individuals.

Mill also says that utility should be distinguished from expediency. Since the utility of an action is determined by the total amount of happiness that is produced by the action, the justness or unjustness of an action may affect its utility. But since the expediency of an action is not necessarily determined by the total amount of happiness that is produced by the action, the justness or unjustness of an action may not necessarily affect its expediency. Actions that conform to the principle of expediency may not necessarily increase the total amount of happiness that is enjoyed by all individuals. On the other hand, actions that conform to the principle of utility must, by definition, increase the total happiness that is enjoyed by all individuals.

Utilitarianism may be divided into three types: 1) act utilitarianism, which asserts that the moral value of an action is determined by whether the action in itself produces the best possible consequences, 2) rule utilitarianism, which asserts that the moral value of an action is determined by whether the action conforms to a rule that tends to produce the best possible consequences, and 3) negative utilitarianism, which asserts that the moral value of an action is determined by whether the action produces less harmful consequences than other actions which could be performed.

Pragmatism is another form of teleological ethics. Ethical pragmatism asserts that the rightness or wrongness of actions is determined not by their motives but by whether they achieve the purposes for which they are performed. Actions are pragmatically right if they have desirable consequences and if they help us to get into a more satisfactory relation with our experiences. Thus, pragmatism may not view any actions as intrinsically right or wrong, because it asserts that actions may be judged only by their consequences.

Intuitionism is another approach to normative ethics, which asserts that proper ethical conduct may be defined by rules or principles that can be known intuitively. Ethical intuitionism affirms that the rightness of wrongness of actions may be known intuitively, even if the consequences of those actions have not been determined.

Henry Sidgwick (1874) describes three phases of ethical intuitionism: 1) perceptional, dogmatic, and 3) philosophical. Perceptional intuitionism affirms that some ethical truths may be intuitively apprehended. Dogmatic intuitionism affirms that some ethical truths may be accepted without being intuitively apprehended. Philosophical intuitionism affirms that some ethical truths may be intuitively apprehended without being undeniably or absolutely self-evident.

Sidgwick explains that insofar as some actions may be judged intuitively to be right or wrong, they may be judged as right or wrong on the basis of their motives or other intrinsic qualities. Intuitionism affirms that some actions may be intrinsically right or wrong, regardless of their consequences. Intuitionism also affirms that some actions may be judged as right or wrong, regardless of how they compare with actions which are required by moral duty.

Virtue Ethics

Virtue ethics is another approach to normative ethics, which differs from the other approaches in focusing on the character of the person who acts, rather than on the character of the actions which that person performs. It is an agent-focused theory rather than an action-focused theory, and it has its origins in ancient Greek philosophy (e.g. Plato and Aristotle) and in ancient Chinese philosophy (e.g. Kongfuzi and Mengzi).[4]

Aristotle distinguishes between two kinds of virtue: 1) moral virtue, and 2) intellectual virtue. Generosity and honesty are examples of moral virtue, while wisdom and understanding are examples of intellectual virtue. Moral virtues are not innate, says Aristotle. They are acquired by means of practice or habit. A person becomes truthful by acting truthfully and becomes unselfish by acting unselfishly. However, it may be more difficult for a person to become virtuous if he has not acquired the habit of acting virtuously. Thus, it may be more difficult for a person to become tactful if he has not acquired the habit of acting tactfully. It may also be more difficult for a person to become unselfish if he has not acquired the habit of acting unselfishly.

In order to perform a morally virtuous action, says Aristotle, an individual must be able to choose how to respond to his own thoughts and feelings. Thus, the concept of moral responsibility implies that an individual has some freedom to choose his own actions. Moral responsibility for an action may be partly determined by whether the action was voluntary or involuntary. An individual may not be morally responsible for having performed an action if he was forced to perform the action involuntarily. He may also not be responsible for having performed the action if he had no control over the action. His personal responsibility for the action may also be determined by whether he had prior knowledge of the possible consequences of the action. His personal responsibli-

---

4. Rosalind Hursthouse, "Virtue Ethics," in *The Stanford Encyclopedia of Philosophy* (online), 2003.

tity may also depend on whether, prior to performing the action, he should have known the possible consequences of the action.

Moral responsibility for an action may also be determined by whether the action is impulsive or deliberate. Impulsive actions may be voluntary, but they may in some cases not be as intentional as more deliberate actions. An individual may have a responsibility to control his own impulses, but if he acts impulsively, he may not be as aware of the possible consequences of his actions as he would be if he acted deliberately.

Aristotle explains that just as an individual may be responsible for his own actions in a given situation, he may also be responsible for his own inaction in that situation. A lack of action by an individual in a given situation may require that individual to accept responsibility for his lack of action. An action in a given situation may also be judged by comparing that action with other actions which the individual could have performed in that same situation.

The moral virtues, according to Aristotle, include courage, temperance, self-discipline, moderation, humility, generosity, honesty, and justice. The moral vices include cowardice, recklessness, wastefulness, self-indulgence, greed, vanity, dishonesty, and injustice. Justice as a moral virtue includes both lawfulness (universal justice) and fairness (particular justice). Injustice as a moral vice includes both unlawfulness and unfairness. Fairness requires that the privileges and responsibilites of individuals in a given situation be distributed proportionally and equally (in order for distributive justice to be achieved). Fairness also requires that an unfair disproportion or inequality in the privileges and responsibilities of individuals in a given situation be rectified (in order for rectificatory justice to be achieved). Rectificatory justice may restore equality or may reallocate privileges and responsibilities to individuals in a given situation. It may also prescribe some form of punishment for individuals who have been unjust, or it may award some form of compensation to those who have been treated unfairly.

Aristotle describes virtue (*arete*) as a principle of temperance and moderation that achieves a mean between the vice of excess and the vice of deficiency of a moral quality. Thus, courage as a moral virtue achieves a mean between recklessness and cowardice. Generosity as a moral virtue achieves a mean between wastefulness and greed. The intellectual virtues include scientific knowledge (*episteme*), artistic or technical knowledge (*techne*), intuitive reason (*nous*), practical reason (*phronesis*), and philosophic wisdom (*sophia*). Scientific knowledge is a knowledge of what is necessary and universal. Technical knowledge is a knowledge of how to make things and of how to develop proficiency in a craft or discipline. Intuitive reason is a process of gaining insight into the first causes of things, and it is a mode of reasoning which establishes the principles of knowledge. Practical wisdom is a capacity to act in accordance with the good of humankind. Philosophic wisdom is a combination of intuitive reason and scientific knowledge.

According to Aristotle, *eudaimonia* (happiness, flourishing, or well-being) is a state of virtuous activity that is guided by the intellect and by reason. It is therefore a contemplative activity. It is not merely a feeling of pleasure or contentment, but a fulfillment of the highest qualities of the human soul. Perfect happiness may be attained by combining practical wisdom (*phronesis*) with theoretical or philosophical wisdom (*sophia*).

Saint Thomas Aquinas (1265) describes virtue as a fullness of ability that is measured by a fitness to act. Virtues are good qualities that dispose us to live rightly and that are given to us by God. Moral virtues include prudence, moderation, courage, and justice. Theological virtues include faith, hope, and charity. Intellectual virtues include wisdom, knowledge, and understanding.

Virtues are not emotions, says Aquinas. Emotions are movements of appetite, but virtues are dispositions of appetite toward movement.[5] Emotions may be good or bad, but virtues dispose us only toward good. In contrast to ordinary dispositions toward good or evil, virtues cannot be misused. They not only enable us to act rightly, but also to choose rightly in making use of that ability to act rightly. Moral virtues dispose us to act according to reason. They are dispositions to choose the right goals and to act appropriately to achieve those goals. Thus, they are based on prudence and understanding.

Prudence is required by the other moral virtues, says Aquinas, but prudence itself requires the other moral virtues. Since the moral virtues are dispositions to make the right choices, they require us not only to aim at the right goals but also to find the right means to attain those goals through the exercise of prudent planning and careful decision making. Prudent planning about the means to achieve our goals, however, presupposes that we have chosen the right goals, and thus it depends on our being disposed toward those goals by the moral virtues.

Of the moral virtues, the cardinal virtues are prudence, moderation, justice, and courage. Prudence is the virtue of being able to exercise care in choosing one's actions. Moderation is the virtue of being able to restrain one's appetites and passions. Justice is the virtue of exchanging and distributing goods according to the principle of fairness and equitability. Courage is the virtue of being able to face up to danger and death.

---

5. St. Thomas Aquinas, *Summa Theologiae: A Concise Translation*, edited by Timothy McDermott (Allen: Christian Classics, 1989), p. 237.

Reason is perfected by the moral, theological, and intellectual virtues. The aim of every virtue is to perfect and strengthen reason, and thus all of the virtues are connected by sharing prudence, which is an ability to reason rightly.[6]

According to Aquinas, virtue may be instilled in us by God or may be acquired through study or habit. Virtues which dispose us to a perfect happiness beyond our own powers are instilled in us by God. God may, however, as a sign of his power, also instill virtues in us which we could have acquired less perfectly through study or habit.

Virtues may be opposed by sin, evil, or vice. Aquinas distinguishes between sins of omission, which may not involve any interior or exterior acts, and sins of commission, which involve interior and/or exterior acts. Sins of omission are acts of failing to do something required by moral duty, while sins of commission are acts of choosing or desiring something morally wrong, or of doing something morally wrong. Sins of omission or commission may be against oneself, against God, or against other human beings.

Aquinas also distinguishes between venial sins, whose harm may be reparable, and mortal sins, whose harm is irreparable. He also distinguishes between sins of the spirit, which are a turning away from God, and sins of the flesh, which are less of a turning away from God, but which are more of a turning toward sensual pleasures. Sins of the flesh may be less voluntary than sins of the spirit.

Some of the harm that sins produce can be foreseen and prevented, says Aquinas. If the harm of a sin is foreseen and not prevented, then the sin is worse, because its harm to those who are affected by it is even more intentional on the part of the sinner. The harm that a sin causes to the sinner himself depends on the gravity of the sin. The worse a sin is, the worse may be the penalty for the sinner.

Sins of ignorance may consist of not knowing what we could or should have known. Ignorance itself is not a sin, says Aquinas, unless it is due to negligence. If there is no way that we can know or could have known something, then ignorance of that thing is not negligent, unless we could or should have recognized and accounted for our ignorance.

Aquinas argues for the existence of original sin, saying that all human beings are born sinful because of the sin committed by Adam and Eve in the Garden of Eden, a sin that has been inherited by all of humankind. If all human beings were not sinful, then there would be no need for us to be redeemed by Christ. Original sin is inherited only by those who are descended from Adam and Eve through the

---

6. *Ibid.*, p. 253.

process of human reproduction. Thus, Jesus had no original sin, as he was conceived of the Holy Spirit and was born of the Virgin Mary.

We cannot overcome sin without God's grace, says Aquinas. We need God's grace in order to refrain from sinning and in order to renew a disposition within ourselves to act rightly. When we sin, we turn away from God. When we repent of our sins, we return to God and are reconciled to him through the mystery of Jesus Christ.

Limitations of Normative Theories

Deontology, consequentialism, intuitionism, and virtue ethics each have their limitations as normative theories.

A major limitation of deontology is that it does not consider the consequences of actions in judging whether they are right or wrong. It may assert that there are moral principles that exist independently of the situations in which moral decisions are made. It may also assert that the validity of moral judgments is determined only by reason and not by experience.

A major limitation of consequentialism is that it does not consider the motives of actions in judging whether they are right or wrong. It may not regard any actions as intrinsically right or wrong, since it judges them only by their consequences. If it regards pleasure as the ultimate good toward which all actions should be aimed, then it may also degenerate into a form of egoistic hedonism. If the happiness of all individuals is defined as the ultimate good toward all actions should be aimed, then it may also fail to explain how this happiness should be distributed among all the individuals who are affected by an action.

A limitation of intuitionism is that it may fail to define any formal principles of conduct. If it asserts that all ethical judgments can be made intuitively, then it may become a form of skepticism regarding rules of conduct. It may not consider any general rules of conduct as useful guidelines for ethical decision making.

A limitation of virtue ethics is that, like intuitionism, it may fail to provide formal rules of conduct. Its focus is on the character of the moral agent, rather than on the interactions which that agent has with other agents. This may lead to uncertainty about the importance of the virtues relative to each other in a given situation, e.g. whether moderation is more important than charity or whether prudence is more important than justice in a given situation.

Christian ethics must, and can, transcend the limitations of all these viewpoints. An adequate system of ethics must consider the motives as well as the consequences of actions in determining whether they are right or wrong. An adequate system of ethics must also provide a means of prioritizing complementary aims or deciding between conflicting aims in various situations. An adequate ethical system must also be applicable to situations in everyday life and must provide a set of guidelines for ethical behavior. An adequate ethical system must also promote ideals such as justice and social harmony that are shared by people of a variety of social and cultural backgrounds.

Ethical Codes

Ethical codes are guidelines for decision making that may enumerate ethical, professional, social, or religious duties and obligations. As codes of duty (deontological codes), they may consist of moral imperatives, rules, or commands. They define the nature of personal responsibility, but they may in some cases also differentiate between what is morally or ethically obligatory and what is desirable or permissible. One of the challenges involved in defining codes of ethics may be to determine whether they can be both prescriptive and generative with respect to ethically desirable conduct.

Ethical codes may define ethical assumptions or principles as well as rules of conduct. Some ethical codes may also prescribe penalties for those who fail to comply with rules of conduct. In order for a code of conduct to function effectively, it must be sufficiently clear and intelligible to those individuals to whom it applies. If it is not sufficiently clear and intelligible, then it may lead to uncertainty about the duties and obligations that have been imposed on individuals.

Some of the characteristics of an effective ethical code may include intelligibility, clarity, consistency, adaptability, wide range of applicability, fidelity to underlying principles or assumptions, and lack of ambiguity. An effective ethical code may also be one with which most individuals who subscribe to it are able to comply, if they sincerely try to comply.

Some important principles of Christian ethics include *humility* ("Judge not, that you be not judged," Matt. 7:1; "Let him who is without sin among you be the first to throw a stone," John 8:7), *forgiveness* ("If any one strikes you on the right cheek, turn to him the other also," Matt. 5:39), *compassion* (exemplified by the Golden Rule, "do unto others as you would have them do unto you"), and *respect for the value of human life and for the value of all living things.*

Ethical duties that are commonly prescribed by Christian ethics include the duty to be concerned about the well-being of other individuals, the duty to promote the well-being of other individuals, the duty not to intentionally harm other individuals, the duty to contribute to the well-being of society, the duty to respect the rights of others, the duty to honor one's parents, the duty to be honest and trustworthy, the duty to keep one's promises, the duty to make amends for wrongful acts, the duty to show gratitude for the kindness of others, the duty to promote justice, the duty to avoid causing unnecessary harm to living things, and the duty to avoid causing unnecessary harm to the environment.

Humility is exemplified by the well-known phrase, "There, but for the grace of God, go I," uttered by the English Protestant reformer and martyr John Bradford (1510-1555) as he watched a group of prisoners being led to the scaffold.

Forgiveness is exemplified by Jesus' words as he suffered on the cross: "Father, forgive them; for they know not what they do" (Luke 23:33).

The Ethical Teachings of Jesus

The ethical teachings of Jesus provide us with a number of rules to follow in everyday life. Some of these rules include: do not kill (Matt. 5:21), do not be angry with your brother (Matt. 5:21), make friends with your enemies (Matt. 5:25), love your enemies (Matt. 5:44), do not commit adultery (Matt 5:27), do not make false promises (Matt. 5:33), show forgiveness to those who trespass against you (Matt. 5:39), give to those who are needy (Matt. 5:42), do not seek to be recognized for your piety (Matt. 6:1), do not be greedy (Matt. 6:24), do not be anxious about material comforts (Matt. 6:25), do not rush to judge other people (Matt. 7:1), correct your own faults before you criticize the faults of others (Matt. 7:3), and act toward others as you would want them to act toward you (Matt. 7:12).

Jesus says explictly that it is his commandment that we love each other as he has loved us (John 15:12). No greater love can be shown for others than to lay down one's life for them (John 15:13).

Jesus also says that we should believe in God, as we believe in him (John 14:1). Those who believe in him believe not in him, but in God, who sent him (John 12:44). We should believe that he is in the Father and that the Father is in him (John 14:11).

Furthermore, Jesus informs us of the most important commandments: "You shall love the Lord your God with all your heart, and with all your soul, and with all your mind. This is the great and first commandment. And a second is like it, you shall love your neighbor as yourself" (Matt. 37-39).

Jesus was thus an ethical teacher as well as a redeemer and savior.[7] He taught us that if we believe in him, and if we follow his example, then we can enter the kingdom of God. He also taught us that the kingdom of God is not coming with signs to be observed; it is already within us, and we have only to look within ourselves to find it (Luke 17:21).

L.H. Marshall (1947) notes that Jesus never suggested that pleasure and pain are valid criteria of right and wrong or that pleasure is the only goal toward which human beings should strive. Thus, Jesus' teachings have nothing to do with utilitarianism. Jesus condemned the self-centered pursuit of pleasure, and he taught the importance of self-sacrfice and altruism.[8]

Christian ethics are both deontological and teleological. They are not only concerned with moral duty, but are also directed toward the perfection of human moral character and the salvation of humankind. They are strict ethics; they teach us that we must strive to be perfect, as our heavenly Father is perfect (Matt. 5:1).

If, as Paul teaches, we are redeemed by faith and not merely by good works (Romans 5:1), then our ethics must promote the moral qualities that will produce those good works.

L.H. Marshall (1947) argues that the ethics of Jesus and St. Paul are not a "code method," but a "spirit method" of ethics; they are primarily concerned with the inner human spirit as the source of moral conduct, and they do not teach that salvation can be attained merely by external obedience to a code of rules. Jesus taught that a sound tree bears good fruit and that a bad tree bears evil fruit (Matt. 7:17-20). Thus human moral conduct is determined by moral character, rather than vice versa. In this respect, says Marshall, Kant's emphasis on the importance of good will is nearer to the central ethical emphasis of Jesus' teachings than other deontological or teleological methods of ethics.[9]

Are religious ethics and philosophical ethics divergent fields of study, or are they complementary to each other? The answer may be that Christian ethics, Jewish ethics, Islamic ethics, Buddhist ethics, and other forms of religious ethics are both religious and philosophical. To try to separate the religious and philosophical aspects may be a futile endeavor. The religious aspects illuminate the philosophical aspects, and the philosophical aspects illuminate the religious aspects.

---

7. L.H. Marshall, *The Challenge of New Testament Ethics* (London: MacMillan & Co., 1964), p. 1.
8. *Ibid.*, p. 9.
9. *Ibid.*, p. 68.

Chapter VII

ETHICS AND LANGUAGE

The Semiotic Dimensions of Ethical Judgments

From a semiotic standpoint, an ethical system may be regarded as a system of signs, and the analysis of an ethical system may be a mode of sign analysis. Ethical semiotics may be a study of ethical signs, and ethical judgments may have syntactic, semantic, and pragmatic dimensions. An ethical judgment may be a sign of agreement or disagreement with an ethical proposition, or it may be a sign of obedience or disobedience to an ethical rule, principle, or code.

Ethical semiotics as an analytic method reveals the interdependence between ethics and language. Ethics may, to some extent, be a mode of language, and language may, to some extent, be a mode of ethics. Thus, ethical semiotics may be concerned not only with the language of ethics, but also with the ethics of language. Ethical judgments may have a logical syntax, and they may, at least to some extent, be governed by linguistic rules of construction.

The Deontic Modality of Ethical Judgments

Deontics may thus provide a means of understanding the relation between ethics and language. Deontics is the study of the deontic modality of linguistic utterances. In order to explore the relation between ethics and deontic modality, it may be useful to review some basic principles of grammar.

Verbs can be classified as *lexical* or *auxiliary*. Lexical verbs can act as the main verb in a verb phrase (e.g. in the sentence,"I washed the car," the verb "washed" is a lexical verb). Auxiliary verbs, on the other hand, accompany the main verb in a verb phrase to express changes in meaning (e.g. in the sentence, "I am washing the car," the verb "am" is auxiliary). Auxiliary verbs are also called "helping verbs." They may be *primary* or *modal*. Primary auxiliaries (e.g. "have," "do," "be") are capable of acting as either lexical verbs or auxiliaries. Modal auxiliaries (e.g. "may," "might," "can," "could," "shall," "should," "will," "would," "must") cannot act as the main verb in a verb phrase.

Verbs can also be classified as *transitive* or *intransitive*. Transitive verbs take a direct object, but intransitive verbs do not. For example, in the sentence, "I washed the car," the noun "car" is a direct object of the transitive verb "washed." In the sentence, "they waited in the lobby," the verb "waited" is intransitive, and the prepositional phrase "in the lobby" acts as an adverb. An object is any noun phrase, other than a subject, that is an argument of a verb.[1] For example, in the sentence, "I sent the letter to her," the noun "letter" is a direct object and the objective personal pronoun "her" is an indirect object of the transitive verb "sent."

Auxiliary verbs include *central modals* ("can," "could," "may," "might," "shall," "should," "will," "would," "must"), *marginal modals* ("dare," "need," "ought to," "used to"), *modal idioms* (e.g. "had better," "would rather"), and *semi-auxiliaries* (auxiliary-like verbs, e.g. "have to," "be able to," "be obliged to," "be willing to").

Modal verbs may have different senses, depending on how they are used. For example, the modals "can" and "could" may indicate possibility, ability, or permission. The modal "must" may indicate obligation or logical necessity. The modals "should" and "ought to" may indicate obligation or tentative inference. The modals "will" and "would" may indicate prediction or volition (intention, willingness, or insistence). The past tense modals "could," "might," and "would" may indicate 1) tentative permission (e.g. in polite requests, such as, "*Could* I have an apple, please?"), 2) tentative volition (e.g. in polite requests, such as, "*Would* you stay here for a moment?"), 3) tentative possibility, in expressing a tentative opinion (e.g. "there *might* be something wrong"), and 4) tentative possibility, in polite directives and requests (e.g. "*Could* you please open the door?").[2]

Possibility and necessity may be expressed not only by modal auxiliaries, but also by lexical modals such as adjectives (e.g. "possible," "necessary," "likely," "probable"), nouns (e.g. "possibility," "necessity," "permission"), and adverbs (e.g. "perhaps," "possibly," "probably," "necessarily," "certainly," "surely").[3]

Auxiliary verbs can carry markings for tense, aspect, and mood. *Tense* is a category of verb inflection that specifies time and duration. The four present tenses are the simple present ("I walk"), the present progressive ("I am walking"), the present perfect ("I have walked"), and the present perfect progressive ("I have been walking"). The four past tenses are the simple past ("I walked"), the past progressive ("I was walking"), the past perfect ("I had walked"), and the past perfect progressive ("I had been walking"). The four future tenses are the simple future ("I will walk"), the future progressive ("I will be walking"), the future perfect ("I will have walked") and the future perfect progressive ("I will have been walking").

---

1. R.L. Trask, *A Student's Dictionary of Language and Linguistics* (London: St. Martin's Press, 1997), p. 155.
2. Randolph Quirk, et al., *A Comprehensive Grammar of the English Language* (London: Longman Group Limited, 1985), pp. 221-233.
3. Rodney Huddleston and Geoffrey K. Pullum, *The Cambridge Grammar of the English Language* (Cambridge: Cambridge University Press, 2002), p. 173.

Aspect is a category of verb inflections that indicate the status of some action or event over a specific period of time (e.g. the sentence, "I am reading the newspaper" indicates that the activity is in progress over a period of time that includes the present moment).

Mood is a grammatical category that indicates the attitude of the speaker toward what he or she is saying, i.e. its degree of certainty, its logical necessity, its believability, its desirability, etc. Mood often involves the use of auxiliary verbs, such as "can," "could," "may," or "might." Moods may be *indicative* (e.g. "you may leave now,"or "did they play cards last night?"), *imperative* (e.g. "take rwo of these tablets"), or *subjunctive* ("I thought that you were leaving").

Modality is a semantic category that may be signaled by mood. The modality of an utterance indicates the speaker's degree of commitment to the certainty, logical necessity, obligatoriness, or desirability of the proposition expressed by the utterance. Modality may be *realis*, *irrealis*, *alethic*, *epistemic*, or *deontic*, but the two main categories are *epistemic* and *deontic*. Realis modality indicates the speaker's estimation of the factuality of the proposition expressed by an utterance (e.g. "the train *will* arrive in two hours"). Irrealis modality indicates the speaker's estimation of the nonfactuality of the proposition expressed by an utterance. (e.g. "you *could not* have finished already"). Alethic modality indicates the speaker's estimation of the logical necessity of the proposition expressed by an utterance (e.g. "Today is Monday, so I *have to* go to work"). Epistemic modality indicates the speaker's degree of certainty about the proposition expressed by an utterance (e.g. "I *might* have made a mistake"). Deontic modality indicates the speaker's degree of commitment to, requirement of, or desire for the actualization of the situation referred to by an utterance (e.g. "you *may* leave now").[4]

Deontic modality may be commissive, directive, or volitive. Commissive modality indicates the speaker's degree of commitment to the actualization of the situation referred to by an utterance. Directive (or imperative) modality indicates the degree to which the speaker demands or requires that the situation referred to by an utterance be actualized. Volitive modality indicates the degree to which the speaker desires for the situation to be actualized.[5]

Sandra Chung and Alan Timberlake (1985) explain that deontic modality may have a number of different senses, depending on its source, target, and

---

4. "Glossary of Linguistic Terms," by Eugene E. Loos (general editor), Susan Anderson (editor), Dwight H. Day, Jr., (editor), Paul C. Jordan (editor), and J. Douglas Wingate (editor), in LinguaLinks Library, online version, SIL International 2004, http://www.sil.org/linguistics/Glossary.

5. *Ibid.*

strength (i.e. speaker's degree of commitment). Its senses include those of being 1) imperative (when the speaker commands the addressee to do something), 2) exhortative (when the speaker exhorts or urges the addressee to do something), 3) voluntative or desiderative (when the speaker expresses an intention to do something), 4) optative (when the speaker desires an action by some participant), 5) jussive (when the speaker allows an event to happen), 6) obligative or debitive (when an action by some participant is required), 7) permissive (when an action by some participant is permitted), and 8) abilitative (when an action is within the ability of some participant). These different senses may be expressed by different moods (indicative, imperative, or subjunctive).[6]

Joan Bybee and Suzanne Fleischman (1995) note that polysemous words such as "may" and "must" may have both deontic and epistemic meanings. For example, the word "may" can be used to express deontic permission (e.g. "you may come in") or epistemic possibility ("this may be your lucky day"), and the word "must" can be used to express deontic obligation ("you must be here by seven o'clock") or inferred probability ("that must be the mailman at the door").[7]

Thus, Bybee (1985) proposes that modal categories be divided into 1) *agent-oriented modality*, including all modal meanings that predicate something about an agent with respect to obligation, desire, ability, permission, or root possibility, 2) *epistemic modality*, indicating a speaker's commitment to the truth of a proposition, and 3) *speaker-oriented modality*, including markers of directives, such as imperatives, optatives, or permissives, through which a speaker attempts to induce an addressee to perform an action. Deontic modality may be agent-oriented or speaker-oriented.[8]

F.R. Palmer (2001) describes two main kinds of modality: 1) *propositional modality* and 2) *event modality*. Propositional modality includes epistemic and evidential modality, while event modality includes deontic and dynamic modality. Epistemic modality may be speculative (e.g. "more people may be coming"), deductive ("more people must be coming"), or assumptive ("more people will be coming"). Evidential modality may be reported (e.g. "he is said to have many important friends") or sensory ("I heard that you were going to be here"). Deon-

---

6. Sandra Chung and Alan Timberlake, "Tense, aspect, and mood," in *Language typology and syntactic description, Volume III: Grammatical categories and the lexicon*, Cambridge: Cambridge University Press, 1985), p. 247.
7. Joan Bybee and Suzanne Fleischman, "Modality in Grammar and Discourse: An Introductory Essay," in *Modality in Grammar and Discourse*, edited by Bybee and Fleischman (Amsterdam: John Benjamins Publishing Company, 1995), p. 5.
8. *Ibid.*, p. 6.

tic modality may be obligative ("you must come in now") or permissive ("you may come in now"). Dynamic modality (which concerns the ability or willingness of someone to do something) may be abilitative (e.g. "she can speak Spanish") or volitive ("I'll call you if I finish before three o'clock").

Deontic Logic

Georg Henrik von Wright (1951), who was a major influence on the development of modal logic (including epistemic logic and deontic logic), explains that some basic axioms of deontic logic can be formulated as follows (using the notation, ~ for negation, & for conjunction, **v** for disjunction, → for material implication, ↔ for material equivalence, PA for A is permitted, and OA for A is obligatory):

1. OA & O(A → B) → OB. (If A is obligatory, and if it is obligatory that if we do A then we must do B, then B is obligatory.)

2. PA & O(A → B) → PB. (If A is permissible, and if it is obligatory that if we do A then we must do B, then B is permissible.)

3. ~PB & O(A → B) → ~PA. (If B is not permissible, and if it is obligatory that if we do A then we must do B, then A is not permissible.)

4. O(A → B **v** C) & ~PB & ~PC → ~PA. (If it is obligatory that if we do A then we must do B or C, and if B is not permissible and C is not permissible, then A is not permissible.)

5. ~(O(A **v** B) & ~PA & ~PB). (It cannot be the case that A or B is obligatory and that A is not permissible and that B is not permissible.)

6. OA & O(A & B → C) → O(B → C). (If A is obligatory, and if it is obligatory that if we do A and B then we must do C, then it is obligatory that if we do B then we must do C.)

7. O(~A → A) → OA. (If it is obligatory that if we do not do A then we must do A, then A is obligatory.)[9]

Some additional axioms in von Wright's system of deontic logic include:

1. Op ↔ ~P ~p. (To say that p is obligatory is materially equivalent to saying that it is not permitted not to do p).

2. P (p **v** q) ↔ Pp **v** Pq. (p or q is permissible if and only if p is permissible or q is permissible.)

---

9. Georg H. von Wright, *An Essay in Modal Logic* (Amsterdam: North-Holland Publishing Company, 1951), pp. 39-40.

3. O (p & q) ↔ Op & Oq. (p and q are obligatory if and only if p is obligatory and q is obligatory.)
4. Op v Oq ⊃ O (p v q). (If p is obligatory or q is obligatory, then p or q is obligatory.)
5. P (p & q) ⊃ Pp & Pq. (If p and q are permissible, then p is permissible and q is permissible.
6. O (p ⊃ q) ⊃ (Op ⊃ Oq). (If it is obligatory that if we do p then we must do q, then if p is obligatory then q is also obligatory.)
7. O (p ⊃ q v r) & ~Pq & ~Pr ⊃ ~Pp. (If it is obligatory that if we do p then we must do q or r, and if q is not permissible and r is not permissible, then p is not permissible.

Another system of deontic logic was later proposed by von Wright, in which the expression "P (p| r)" may be read as "p is permissible under circumstances r."[10] Thus, some additional axioms are

1. P (p v q | r) ≡ P (p | r) v P (q | r). (p or q are permissible under circumstances r if and only if p is permissible under circumstances r or q is permissible under circumstances r.)

2. ~[O (A |B) & O (~ A | B)]. (It cannot be the case that A is obligatory under circumstances B and that not-A is obligatory under the same circumstances B.)

3. O (p | r v s) ⊃ O (p | r) & O (p | s). (If p is obligatory under circumstances r or s, then p is obligatory under circumstances r and p is obligatory under circumstances s.)

Categories of Deontic Modality

Ethical judgments include judgments about deontic modality, i.e. they include judgments about 1) what we *must* do or what rightly *must* happen in a given situation, 2) what we *should* (or *ought to*) do or what rightly *should* (or *ought to*) happen in a given situation, 3) what we rightly *may* do or what rightly *may* happen in a given situation, 4) what we rightly *may not* do or what rightly *may not* happen in a given situation, 5) what we *should not* do or what rightly *should not* happen in

---

10. Dagfinn Føllesdal and Risto Hilpinen, "Deontic Logic: An Introduction," in *Deontic Logic: Introductory and Systematic Readings*, edited by Risto Hilpinen (Dordrecht: D. Reidel Publishing Company, 1971), p. 27.

a given situation, and 6) what we *must not* do or what rightly *must not* happen in a given situation. Ethical judgments may therefore include 1) imperatives or commands, 2) prescriptions, 3) permissions, 4) non-permissions, 5) admonitions, and 6) proscriptions or prohibitions.

Moral imperatives or commands tell us what we must do or what rightly must happen in a given situation. They inform us of our duties and obligations. They may be hypothetical or categorical, conditional or unconditional.

Moral prescriptions (teachings, instructions, advisements) tell us what we should do or what rightly should happen in a given situation. An action that is prescribed may also be obligatory, but it may, in some cases, be non-obligatory (i.e. not absolutely required).

Moral options or permissions tell us what actions are acceptable or permissible in a given situation. Actions that are permissible may not necessarily be advisable or obligatory. However, they are acceptable, even if they do not strictly conform to prescriptions or commands. They may also in some cases exceed moral obligation or duty. Actions that try to resolve conflicts between competing obligations or between competing standards of duty may be permissible without necessarily being prescribed or obligatory.

If an action is not morally obligatory, then it may be merely recommended, merely permissible, morally indifferent, or impermissible. If an action is not recommended within the context of a moral system, then it cannot be obligatory, but it may be permissible, morally indifferent, or impermissible. If an action is impermissible within the context of a moral system, then it cannot be recommended or obligatory.

In order for an action to be morally obligatory, it must at least be permissible and recommended. In order for an action to be morally impermissible, it must at least be non-obligatory and not necommended.

Gratuitous actions may include those that are unnecessary and that are without justification. Depending on whether they are in conflict with moral commands, prescriptions, or permissions, they may be morally permissible, indifferent, or impermissible.

Unjustified actions include those that are unnecessary but acceptable, those that are unnecessary and unacceptable, and those that are acceptable but not recommended due to lack of grounds. Justified actions include those that are acceptable, recommended, or obligatory.

Some moral judgments may be about actions or situations that are neither right nor wrong. Morally indifferent actions may be those that are neither required nor forbidden, neither recommended nor disapproved, neither formally recognized as acceptable nor formally recognized as unacceptable. Such actions may not be able to be judged by standards of moral obligation or duty. However, it is open to question whether any moral judgments can ever be completely indifferent (neither right nor wrong).

It is also open to question whether an adequate ethical code can consist only of imperatives or commands. If our ethical judgments include not only decisions about what we must or must not do, but also decisions about what we should or should not do (and what we rightly may or may not do), then an adequate ethical code may need to include not only commands, but also prescriptions, permissions, admonitions, and prohibitions.

Codes consisting predominantly of moral commands may be more "legalistic" than codes consisting predominantly of moral permissions, while codes consisting predominantly of moral permissions may be more "permissive" or "intuitionistic" than codes consisting predominantly of moral commands.

For the class of codes that contain moral permissions and prescriptions as well as commands, some may be more permissive than others, depending on the number, variety, and extent of moral permissions that they contain.

Morally "right" actions include those actions that are more obligatory than others in a given situation. Thus, morally obligatory actions are "better" or "more right" to perform in a given situation than actions that are merely recommended or permissible. Failure to perform actions that are morally obligatory is "more wrong" than failure to perform actions that are merely acceptable or recommended.

W.D. Ross (1930) explains that when the term "right" is used to describe moral conduct, it may be ambiguous, because it may refer to both the quality of being morally obligatory and the quality of being morally good. Actions that are morally obligatory may not necessarily be morally good. For example, morally obligatory actions that are performed solely for the sake of expediency may not necessarily be morally good. Actions that do not have good motives may be morally "right" if they conform to duty, but they may not necessarily be morally "good."

Ross also explains that the term "good" may be used in a variety of senses. For example, in the sentence, "he is a good card player," the word "good" is used attributively to mean "skillful" or "successful." In the sentence, "this is a good knife," the word "good" is used attributively to mean "useful" or "efficient." In the sentence, "knowledge is good," the word "good" is used predicatively to mean "desirable" or "admirable."

Ross argues that virtuous action is motivated not only by the desire to do what is morally right (i.e. what is required by moral duty), but also by the desire to produce some form of good. The moral value of an action is determined by whether the action has good motives and by whether the action is intended to produce some form of good.

Moral codes that consist predominantly of commands may be more explicit in what they require than codes that consist predominantly of prescriptions and permissions. Codes may need to have a certain degree of explicitness in order for individuals to comply with them. However, codes that consist exclusively of commands may sacrifice flexibility and adaptability in order to gain unequivocality. On the other hand, codes that consist predominantly of permissions may sacrifice unequivocality in order to gain flexibility and adaptability. Every moral code must have some imperatives and some absolute prohibitions; otherwise, no mode of conduct will be obligatory and no mode of conduct will be impermissible.

Moral codes may themselves require rules of application, rules of change, and rules of reordering or reconfiguration. These secondary rules may determine how moral codes are integrated into other codes (social and cultural).

Conscience may often be prescriptive in character, insofar as it reflects on actions that should or should not have been performed. It may prescribe compliance with duty, or it may prescribe atonement for acts of noncompliance with duty. Failures of conscience may result in denial of duty, neglect of duty, or further noncompliance with duty.

Moral certainty may depend on the existence and unequivocality of moral commands, prescriptions, permissions, non-permissions, admonitions, and prohibitions. It may also depend on their stability, range of application, utility, and justifiability.

Moral uncertainty may be caused by ambiguity, vagueness, or equivocality of commands, and by difficulty assigning priority to one command over another. It may also be caused by unexpected changes in the urgency of moral commands or prescriptions. Uncertainty may occur if moral permissions unexpectedly become prescriptions, or if prescriptions unexpectedly become commands.

Moral certainty or uncertainty may also depend of how rigidly or flexibly, conscientiouslessly or unconscientiously, consistently or inconsistenty the rules of a moral code are applied.

However, moral judgments include not only judgments about rules of conduct, but also judgments about good and evil, about right and wrong. We must therefore look for some guidance in Jesus' teachings to help us decide how to make these judgments, and we must also try to develop a clearer understanding of what should be the ultimate goal of our moral conduct.

Christian Love as an Ethical Language

One possible answer to the question of what should be the goal of moral conduct is that we should try to follow Jesus' example of obedience to God's will. We should dedicate ourselves to relieving human suffering and to promoting the well-being of humankind. We should try to model our lives according to Jesus' life and teachings. We should strive to be like Jesus in our hearts, in our minds, and in our actions.

Jesus tells us to believe in him and to believe in God (John 14:1). He tells us that those who believe in him will act as he acts (John 14:12). He also says that it is his commandment that we love each other as he has loved us (John 15:12). Paul also tells us that we should love each other as God loves us. Faith, hope, and love should dwell in our hearts, but love is the greatest of these virtues (1 Cor. 13:13), and we should strive to express it in our lives.

The First Letter of John also tells us that to know God is to know love, because God is love. The love of God was made manifest to us when God sent his only Son into the world, so that we might live through him. God so loved us that he sent his only Son to be the expiation for our sins. If God so loved us, then we also should love one another. God's love dwells in us when we love one another, and his perfect love can be revealed through us (4:8-12).

Chapter VIII

CONCLUSION

Fields of Study for Theological Semiotics

Christianity, Judaism, Islam, Buddhism, Hinduism, and other religions may be fields of study for theological semiotics.

In Islamic semiotics, the Arabic word "*ayah*," meaning "sign," is the term for a verse in the Qur'an. Thus, each verse in the Qur'an is a sign through which the word of God is conveyed to humankind.[1] The Arabic word "Islam" means submission, i.e. submission to the will of God. Other signs include the five pillars of Islam: 1) the *shahada* (profession of faith), 2) the *salat* (daily prayers), 3) the *zakat* (almsgiving), 4) the *sawm* (fasting during the month of Ramadan), and 5) the *hajj* (pilgrimage to Mecca).

Other sacred signs in Islam include the six articles of faith: 1) belief in God (*tawhid*), 2) belief in the angels (*mala'ika*), 3) belief in God's revealed books (*kutub*), 4) belief in the prophets (*nabi*) and messengers (*rusul*), 5) belief in the day of judgment (*qiyima*), and 6) belief in divine predestination (*qadar*).

Sacred Islamic shrines include the Ka'ba in Mecca, the Mosque of the Prophet Muhammad in Medina, and the Dome of the Rock in Jerusalem.

The wearing of a veil (*hijab*) can have a multidimensional symbolism for Muslim women. It may express attitudes or beliefs about religious faith, about moral conduct, about the responsibilities of women, about obedience to religious authority, and about the importance of religion in modern society.

Islamic festivals include Eid-al-Fitr (the festival that occurs at the end of the month of Ramadan) and Eid-al-Adha (the festival that occurs at the end of the *hajj* and that celebrates Abraham's willingness to obey the will of God).

In Jewish semiotics, the *mezuzah* is a small encased parchment scroll, inscribed with passages from the Torah, which is hung from each doorpost of a Jewish home, symbolizing G-d's presence and the family's obedience to G-d's *mitzvot* (commandments). Other Jewish symbols include the *menorah* (an eight-branched candelabrum used during the festival of Chanukkah to commemorate the miracle of the jar of oil; the jar in the Temple of Jerusalem contained only enough oil for one day, but it kept the eternal flame alight for eight days, until the rebuilding of the temple was completed).

Another sacred symbol of Judaism is the Western Wall in Jerusalem, the remains of the Second Temple that was destroyed by the Romans in 70 C.E. Jews

---

1. *Dictionary of Semiotics*, edited by Thomas Sebeok (Berlin: Mouton de Gruyter, 1994), p. 392.
   Atzmaut (Israeli Independence Day), Yom Ha Zikkaron (Israeli Memoiral Day), Yom Yerushalayim (Jerusalem Day), Shav'ot, and Tisha B'Av.

go to the Western Wall to pray and to read from the Torah, and it is a site of pilgrimage for Jews from around the world.

Other sacred symbols include the *yarmulke* (the skullcap symbolizing respect for G-d), the star of David, the *talis* (the prayer shawl), and the *shofar* (the ram's horn that is blown in the temple on Yom Kippur, signaling the end of fasting).

Jewish holidays include Rosh Hashanah (Jewish New Year), Yom Kippur (day of atonement), Chanukkah (festival of lights), Passover (commemorating the Exodus from Egypt), Sukkot (festival of booths), and Shemini Atzeret/Simchat Torah (holidays after Sukkot).

In Tibetan Buddhism, the "eight auspicious symbols" (*ashtamangala*) are 1) the parasol, representing protection from evil, 2) two golden fish, representing salvation from suffering, 3) the treasure vase, representing spiritual fulfillment, 4) the lotus, representing purity, 5) the conch shell, symbolizing the sound of the Dharma (Buddha's teachings), 6) the endless knot, symbolizing the infinite wisdom of the Buddha, 7) the victory banner, symbolizing the victory of the Dharma, and 8) the wheel, representing the wheel of law (the teachings of the Buddha).

Buddhist wheel symbols include the *dharmachakra* (wheel of the law) and the *bhavachakra* (wheel of life). The *dharmachakra* has a rim, representing concentration; eight spokes, representing the eightfold path of righteousness; and a hub, representing spiritual discipline. The *bhavachakra* has a rim divided into twelve sections, representing the twelve causes of cyclic existence, a central portion divided into six sections, representing the six worlds (the world of *devas* or divine beings, the world of *asuras* or fighting demons, the world of humans, the world of animals, the world of *pretas* or hungry ghosts, and the world of hell), and a hub decorated with three animals (a pig, a snake, and a rooster), symbolizing the three poisons (greed, hatred, and delusion).

In Buddhist art, images of the Buddha usually have a protuberance on top of the head (symbolizing wisdom), elongated earlobes (symbolizng wisdom and spiritual advancement), half-closed eyes and a gentle smile (representing serenity), characteristic hand gestures (or *mudras*, symbolizing earth-touching, explanation, fearlessness, prayer, meditation, or wisdom), and bodily postures (sitting, standing, or reclining) symbolizing enlightenment and spiritual perfection.

Other symbols of Buddhism include monks' robes, prayer beads, prayer wheels, incense burners, thunderbolt scepters, lotus thrones and pedestals, mandalas (cosmological diagrams), stupas, and pagodas.

Buddhism has many forms of number symbolism. For example, the three jewels or refuges are 1) the Budhha, 2) the Dharma, and 3) the Sangha (the monastic community). The three bodies of the Buddha are 1) the truth body (*dharmakaya*), 2) the body of bliss (*sambhogakaya*), and 3) the emanation body (*nirmanakaya*). The three characteristics of existence are 1) suffering (*dukkha*), 2) impermanence (*anicca*), and 3) absence of permanent self (*anatta*). The three doors of liberation are 1) emptiness (*shunyata*), 2) signlessness (*animitta*), and 3) aimlessness (*apranihita*). The four noble truths are of 1) the pervasiveness of suffering, 2) the causes of suffering, 3) the cessation of suffering, and 4) the path to the cessation of suffering. The four immeasurable minds are 1) love (*metta*), 2) compassion (*karuna*), 3) joy (*mudita*), and 4) equanimity (*upekkha*). The five *skandhas* (or aggregates of existence) are 1) form (*rupa*), 2) feeling (*vedana*), 3) perception (*samjna*), 4) impulses (*samskaras*), and 5) consciousness (*vijnana*). The five hindrances (*kleshas*) are 1) anger, 2) craving, 3) ignorance, 4) jealousy, and 5) pride. The five precepts for Buddhist laypeople are 1) refrain from taking life, 2) refrain from stealing, 3) refrain from sexual misconduct, 4) refrain from false or idle speech, and 5) refrain from drugs or alcohol that cloud the mind. The six *paramitas* (perfections) are 1) generosity (*dana*), 2) morality (*shila*), 3) patience (*kshanti*), 4) perseverence (*virya*), 5) meditation (*dhyana*), and 6) wisdom (*prajna*). The eight paths of righteousness are 1) right views (*samma-ditthi*), 2) right intentions (*samma-sankappa*), 3) right speech (*samma-vaca*), 4) right action (*samma-kammanta*), 5) right livelihood (*samma-ajiva*), 6) right effort (*samma-vayama*), 7) right mindfulness (*samma-sati*), and 8) right concentration (*samma-samadhi*).

Buddhism teaches that signs are the outer appearances of things. Signs are often misleading, and we must learn to distinguish outer appearance from true reality. Signlessness (*animitta*) is the second door of liberation. To understand the true nature of reality is to understand the signlessness of signs. Right concentration enables us to go beyond the outer appearances or signs of things, and it is a means of freeing ourselves from falsehood and misperception.

Hindu symbols include the sacred syllable "Aum" (representing Brahman), *vibhuti* (holy ash drawn across the forehead in three horizontal lines, representing Shiva), the *bindi* (the decorative red dot worn on the forehead by married Hindu women), the lotus (a symbol of purity and creation), the banyan tree (a symbol of life and immortality), the cow (a symbol of purity and nonviolence), and the Ganges River (whose waters are believed to be sacred).

Hindu scriptures include the Vedas, the Upanishads (which form the final portion of the Vedas), the Brahma Sutras, the Ramayana, the Mahabharata (whose sixth book contains the Bhaghavad Gita), and the Puranas.

In Hindu iconography, each deity has a characteristic vehicle (*vahana*) on which he or she is seated, and which symbolizes one of his or her attributes. For Agni, it is a ram. For Brahma, it is a swan. For Durga, it is a lion or tiger. For Indra, it is an elephant. For Shiva, it is Nandi, the bull. For Varuna, it is a fish. For Vishnu, it is Garuda, a mythical bird. For Yama, it is a buffalo.

Hindu festivals include Diwali (or Deepavali, the festival of lights), Durga Puja (or Navaratri, honoring Durga), Ganesh Chaturthi (honoring Ganesh, the elephant-headed god of wisdom), Krishna Janmashtami (celebrating the birthday of Krishna), Raksha Bandham (a family festival in which sisters present their brothers with a sacred thread), Holi (commemorating the love of Krishna and Radha), and Shivaratri (honoring Shiva).

Viewpoints that religions may take toward each other include those of exclusivism, inclusivism, or pluralism. While there may be many ways of defining these viewpoints, one way might be to say that exclusivism holds that there is only one true path to God and only one way to attain salvation; inclusivism holds that there is only one true path to God, but that there is more than one way of following this path and consequently more than one way of attaining salvation; and pluralism holds that there may be many different paths leading to God and therefore many different ways of attaining salvation. To say that various religions may be fields of study for theological semiotics is not necessarily to adopt any one of these three viewpoints.

Religions may differ in their uses of symbolism and in their ways of assigning meaning to symbols. They may also differ in their ways of interpreting signs and symbols. They may also differ in the degree of importance that they attach to icons, images, and symbols.

Limitations and Strengths of Theological Semiotics

What are the limitations of semiotics as a method of investigating the nature of religious faith and worship? The answer may lie in the limitations of linguistic signs and symbols as a means of expressing our thoughts and feelings. The subjects with which religious faith is concerned (God, ultimate reality, the first cause of all things, the sacred, etc.) may transcend the limits of language.

There is also the question of whether the way in which we use theological language is determined by the way in which we think about God, or whether the way in which we think about God is determined by the way in which we use theological language. This is the question that was confronted by Ludwig Wittgenstein (1921), the question of whether the way in which we use language is determined by the way in which we perceive the world, or whether the way in which we perceive the world is determined by the way in which we use language.

Wittgenstein says that the limits of language are also the limits of what we can think, and that we cannot think about things than cannot be put into language. However, Stephen David Ross (1994) takes an opposing viewpoint. There is nothing that cannot be put into language, says Ross, but there is also nothing that can be put into language completely. There is always something more to be said about whatever we want to talk about. Thus, the inexhaustibility of things that can be said imposes a profound ethical responsbility upon us regarding our use of language.[2]

On the one hand, it can be argued that God's infinity overflows the capacity of any signifier to represent it. On the other hand, it can be argued that if language is inexhaustible as a means of expressing our thoughts and feelings, then there is also an inexhaustible number of ways in which we can think about God and an inexhaustible number of ways in which we can express these thoughts symbolically.

Symbolism is ubiquitous in Christian religious, social, and aesthetic expression. Study of the meaning, function, uses, purposes, and effects of symbolism may enable us to gain a better understanding of the multiple ways in which people can express their religious faith. For example, discourse analysis may enable us to gain a greater understanding of the similarities and differences between Christianity in Africa, Asia, Europe, and Central and South America.

If we explore the meaning of religious symbols, then perhaps we can also develop a greater appreciation of the similarities and differences in the belief systems of people of various religious faiths. One of the greatest challenges that humankind faces is the task of enabling individuals of different cultural, racial, ethnic, and religious backgrounds to coexist peacefully and to communicate effectively with each other. Study of Christianity, Islam, Judaism, Buddhism, or Hinduism as modes of religious discourse may include both synchronic and diachronic, both syntagmatic and paradigmatic, both structural and relational analysis of discursive practices and may be a means of promoting wider and more open interfaith dialogue.

---

2. Stephen David Ross, *The Limits of Language* (New York: Fordham University Press, 1994), p. 23.

BIBLIOGRAPHY

Aquinas, St. Thomas. *Summa Theologiae: A Concise Translation.* Edited by Timothy McDermott. Allen, Texas: Christian Classics, 1989.

Aristotle. "Ethica Nicomachea." Translated by W.D. Ross, in *The Basic Works of Aristotle.* Edited by Richard McKeon. New York: Random House, 1941.

Augustine, Saint. *On Christian Doctrine.* Translated by D.W. Robertson, Jr. New York: Macmillan Publishing Company, 1958.

Augustine, Saint. *The Works of Saint Augustine: A Translation for the 21st Century.* Translated by Edmund Hill. Hyde Park: New City Press, 2005.

Austin, J.L. *How to do things with Words.* Cambridge: Harvard University Press, 1962.

Bakhtin, Mikhail. *The Bakhtin Reader.* Edited by Pam Morris. London: Arnold, 1994.

Barth, Karl. *Church Dogmatics. Volume I: The Doctrine of the Word of God.* Translated by G.W. Bromiley. Edinburgh: T. & T. Clark, 1975.

Barthes, Roland. *Elements of Semiology.* Translated by Annette Lavers and Colin Smith. New York: Hill and Wang, 1964.

Barthes, Roland. "Textual Analysis: Poe's Valdemar," in *Modern Criticism and Theory: A Reader.* Edited by David Lodge. London: Longman (1988), pp. 172-94.

Barthes, Roland. *S/Z.* Translated by Richard Miller. New York: Hill and Wang, 1974.

Baudrillard, Jean. *Simulacra and Simulation.* Translated by Sheila Faria Glaser. Ann Arbor: The University of Michigan Press, 1994.

Biblical Revelation and Inclusive Language: A Report of the Commission on Theology and Church Relations of the Lutheran Church-Missouri Synod, February 1998. St. Louis: The Lutheran Church-Missouri Synod, 1996.

Buber, Martin. *I and Thou*. Translated by Ronald Gregor Smith. New York: Charles Scribner's Sons, 1958.

Bultmann, Rudolf. "New Testament and Mythology," in *Kerygma and Myth: A Theological Debate*. Edited by Hans Werner Bartsch. Translated by Reginald H. Fuller. London: S.P.C.K. (1953), pp. 1-44.

Bybee, Joan and Fleischman, Suzanne. "Modality in Grammar and Discourse: An Introductory Essay," in *Modality in Grammar and Discourse*, edited by Bybee and Fleischman. Amsterdam: John Benjamins Publishing Company (1995), pp. 1-14.

Bybee, Joan L. *Morphology: A Study of the Relation between Meaning and Form*. Amsterdam: John Benjamins Publishing Company, 1985.

Campbell, Joseph. *The Hero with a Thousand Faces*. New York: Pantheon Books, 1949.

Chandler, Daniel. *Semiotics: The Basics*. Abingdon: Routledge, 2002.

Chomsky, Noam. *Aspects of the Theory of Syntax*. Cambridge: The M.I.T. Press, 1965.

Chomsky, Noam. *Rules and Representations*. New York: Columbia University Press, 1980.

Chopp, Rebecca S. *The Power to Speak: Feminism, Language, God*. New York: Crossroad Publishing Company, 1989.

Chung, Sandra and Timberlake, Alan. "Tense, aspect, and mood," in *Language typology and syntactic description, Volume III: Grammatical categories and the lexicon*. Cambridge: Cambridge University Press, 1985), p. 247.

Corbett, Edward P.J. *Classical Rhetoric for the Modern Student*. New York: Oxford University Press, 1990.

Crystal, David. *A Dictionary of Linguistics and Phonetics*. Oxford: Basil Blackwell Ltd., 1980.

Daly, Mary. *Beyond God the Father: Toward a Philosophy of Women's Liberation*. Boston: Beacon Press, 1973.

Dante Alighieri. *The Comedy of Dante Alighieri, the Florentine. Cantica I: Hell (L'Inferno)*. Translated by Dorothy L. Sayers. Harmondworth: Penguin Books, 1949.

Dante Alighieri. *The Divine Comedy of Dante Alighieri: Inferno*. Translated by Allen Mandelbaum. New York: Bantam Books, 1980.

Dante Alighieri. *The Comedy of Dante Alighieri, the Florentine. Cantica II: Purgatory (Il Purgatorio)*. Translated by Dorothy L. Sayers. Harmondsworth: Penguin Books, 1955.

Dante Alighieri. *The Comedy of Dante Alighieri, the Florentine. Cantica III: Paradise (Il Paradiso)*. Translated by Dorothy L. Sayers and Barbara Reynolds. Harmondsworth: Penguin Books, 1962.

Darwall, Stephen. *Philosophical Ethics*. Boulder: Westview Press, 1998.

Derrida, Jacques. *Of Grammatology*. Translated by Gayatri Chakravorty Spivak. Baltimore: The Johns Hopkins University Press, 1974.

Dominican Fathers, The. *How to Pray the Rosary*. Portland: The Rosary Center, 2006, online http://www.pacifier.com.

Eco, Umberto. *A Theory of Semiotics*. Bloomington: Indiana University Press, 1979.

Fergusson, Francis. *Dante*. New York: The MacMillan Company, 1966.

Føllesdal, Dagfinn and Hilpinen, Risto. "Deontic Logic: An Introduction," in *Deontic Logic: Introductory and Systematic Readings*. Edited by Risto Hilpinen. Dordrecht: D. Reidel Publishing Company, 1971).

Foucault, Michel. *The Archaeology of Knowledge*. Translated by A.M. Sheridan Smith. New York: Pantheon Books, 1972.

Gadamer, Hans-Georg. *Truth and Method.* New York: The Seabury Press, 1975.

Genette, Gérard. *Narrative Discourse Revisited.* Translated by Jane E. Lewin. Ithaca: Cornell University Press, 1988.

Greimas, A.J. and Courtés, J. *Semiotics and Language: An Analytical Dictionary.* Bloomington: Indiana University Press, 1979).

Halliday, M.A.K. and Hasan, Ruqaiya. *Cohesion in English.* Hong Kong: Longman Co. Ltd., 1976.

Hanh, Thich Nhat. *The Heart of the Buddha's Teachings.* New York: Broadway Books, 1998.

Harris, Zelig. "Discourse Analysis," in *The Structure of Language: Readings in the Philosophy of Language.* Edited by Jerry A. Fodor and Jerrold J. Katz. Englewood Cliffs: Prentice-Hall (1964), pp. 355-83.

Harrison, Randall P. *Beyond Words: An Introduction to Nonverbal Communication.* Englewood Cliffs: Prentice-Hall, 1974.

Hartmann, Nicolai. *Möglichkeit und Wirklichkeit*, Second Edition. Berlin: Walter de Gruyter, 1949.

Hjelmslev, Louis. *Prolegomena to a Theory of Language.* Madison: University of Wisconsin Press, 1963.

Huddleston, Rodney and Pullum, Geoffrey K. *The Cambridge Grammar of the English Language.* Cambridge: Cambridge University Press, 2002.

Hursthouse, Rosalind. "Virtue Ethics." in *The Stanford Encyclopedia of Philosophy* (online), 2003.

Jakobson, Roman. "Closing Statement: Linguisitcs and Poetics," in *Style in Language.* Edited by Thomas A. Sebeok. Cambridge: The M.I.T. Press (1960), pp. 350-377.

Kant, Immanuel. *Groundwork of the Metaphysic of Morals.* Translated by H.J. Paton. New York: Harper & Row, 1964.

Kennedy, Richard. *The International Dictionary of Religion*. New York: The Crossroad Publishing Company, 1984.

Kieckhefer, Richard. *Theology in Stone: Church Architecture from Byzantium to Berkeley*. Oxford: Oxford University Press, 2004.

Knapp, Mark L. and Hall, Judith A. *Nonverbal Communication in Human Interaction*. Fort Worth: Holt, Rinehart and Winston 1992.

Kristeva, Julia. *Desire in Language: A Semiotic Approach to Literature and Art*. Edited by Leon S. Roudiez. Translated by Thomas Gora, Alice Jardine, and Leon S. Roudiez. New York: Clumbia University Press, 1980.

Kuhns, Elizabeth. *The Habit: A History of the Clothing of Catholic Nuns*. New York: Doubleday, 2003.

Lakoff, George and Johnson, Mark. *Metaphors We Live By*. Chicago: The University of Chicago Press, 1980.

Lakoff, George and Turner, Mark. *More than Cool Reason: A Field Guide to Poetic Metaphor*. Chicago: The University of Chicago Press, 1989.

Lakoff, George and Johnson, Mark. *Philosophy in the Flesh: The Embodied Mind and its Challenge to Western Thought*. New York: Basic Books, 1999.

Langan, Janine. "The Christian Imagination," in *The Christian Imagination*. Edited by Leland Ryken. Colorado Springs: Shaw Books (2002), pp. 63-80.

Langer, Susanne K. *Philosophy in a New Key: A Study in the Symbolism of Reason, Rite, and Art*. Cambridge: Harvard University Press, 1942.

Larousse Biographical Dictionary. Edited by Magnus Magnusson. Edinburgh: Larousse, 1994.

Lévi-Strauss, Claude. *Structural Anthopology*. Translated by Claire Jacobson and Brooke Schoepf. New York: Basic Books, 1963.

Loberger, Gordon and Welsh, Kate Shoup. *Webster's New World English Grammar Handbook*. New York: Hungry Minds, 2001.

Longman III, Tremper. "Biblical Poetry," in *A Complete Literary Guide to the Bible*. Edited by Leland Ryken and Tremper Longman III. Grand Rapids: Zondervan Publishing House (1993), pp. 80-91.

Loos, Eugene E. "Glossary of Linguistic Terms," by Eugene E. Loos (general editor), Susan Anderson (editor), Dwight H. Day, Jr., (editor), Paul C. Jordan (editor), and J. Douglas Wingate (editor). "Glossary of Linguistic Terms, in *LinguaLinks Library*, online version, SIL International 2004, http://www.sil.org/linguistics/Glossary.

Luther, Martin. "Sermon for the Second Sunday in Advent. Luke 21:25-36. The Signs of the Day of Judgment," in *The Sermons of Martin Luther. Volume I*. Grand Rapids: Baker Book House, (1983), pp. 59-83.

Lyons, John. *Linguistic Semantics: An Introduction*. Cambridge: Cambridge University Press, 1995.

Marshall, L.H. *The Challenge of New Testament Ethics*. London: MacMillan & Co. 1964.

McArthur, Meher. *Reading Buddhist Art: An Illustrated Guide to Buddhist Signs and Symbols*. London: Thames & Hudson Ltd., 2002.

McGrath, Alister E. *Christian Theology: An Introduction*. Oxford: Blackwell, 1994.

McGrath, Alister E., editor. *The Christian Theology Reader*. Oxford: Blackwell, 1995.

Mill, J.S. *Utilitarianism*. Edited by Roger Crisp. Oxford: Oxford University Press, 1998.

Milton, John. *Paradise Lost*. Edited by Merritt Y. Hughes. New York: Odyssey Press, 1962.

Milton, John. "De Doctrina Christiana," in *The Works of John Milton*, Volume XIV. Translated by Charles R. Sumner. New York: Columbia University Press, 1933.

Milton, John. "The Tenure of Kings and Magistrates," in *The Works of John Milton*, Volume V. New York: Columbia University Press, 1933.

Morris, Charles W. *Writings on the General Theory of Signs*. The Hague: Mouton, 1971.

Nöth, Winfried. *Handbook of Semiotics*. Bloomington: Indiana University Press, 1990.

Ogden, C.K. and Richards, I.A. *The Meaning of Meaning: A Study of the Influence of Language upon Thought and of the Science of Symbolism*. New York: Harcourt, Brace & Company, 1925.

Palmer, F.R. *Mood and Modality*. Cambridge: Cambridge University Press, 2001.

Peirce, Charles Sanders. *Collected Papers of Charles Sanders Peirce*. Volumes I and II. Cambridge: Harvard University Press, 1960.

Peirce, Charles Sanders. *Collected Papers of Charles Sanders Peirce*. Volumes V and VI. Cambridge: Harvard University Press, 1960.

Peirce, Charles Sanders. *Collected Papers of Charles Sanders Peirce*. Volume VIII. Cambridge: Harvard University Press, 1958.

Pike, Kenneth L. *Linguistic Concepts: An Introduction to Tagmemics*. Lincoln: University of Nebrask Press, 1982.

Pope Pius XII. *Mystici Corporis Christi* (*On the Mystical Body of Christ*). Irondale: EWTN, 1999.

Prieto, Luis J. *Messages et signaux*. Paris: Presses Universitaires. 1966.

Quirk, Randolph, et al. *A Comprehensive Grammar of the English Langauge*. London: Longman Group Ltd., 1985.

Richards, I.A. *The Philosophy of Rhetoric*. New York: Oxford University Press, 1965.

Ricoeur, Paul. *The Symbolism of Evil*. Translated by Emerson Buchanan. Boston: Beacon Press, 1967.

Ross, W.D. *The Right and the Good*. Oxford: Oxford University Press, 1930.

Ross, Stephen David. *The Limits of Language*. New York: Forham University Press, 1994.

Saussure, Ferdinand de. *Course in General Linguistics*. Edited by Charles Bally and Albert Sechehaye, in collaboration with Albert Riedlinger. Translated by Wade Baskin. New York: McGraw-Hill Book Company, 1966.

Schillebeeckx, Edward. *The Eucharist*. New York: Burns & Oates, 1968.

Searle, John R. "A classification of illocutionary acts," in *Language in Society*, Vol. 5 (1976), 10-16.

Searle, John R. and Daniel Vanderveken. *Foundations of Illocutionary Logic*. Cambridge: Cambridge University Press (1985), 7-21.

Sebeok, Thomas A. *Signs: An Introduction to Semiotics*. Toronto: University of Toronto Press, 1994.

"The Seven Ecumenical Councils of the Undivided Church," translated by H.R. Percival, in *Nicene and Post-Nicene Fathers*, 2nd Series. Edited by P. Schaff and H. Wace. Grand Rapids: Wm. B. Eerdmans (1955), XIV, pp. 543-4.

Shepherd, Rowena and Rupert. *1000 Symbols*. New York: Thames & Hudson, 2002.

Sidgwick, Henry. *The Methods of Ethics*. Indianapolis: Hackett Publishing Company, 1981.

Thielicke, Helmut. "The Restatement of New Testament Mythology," in *Kerygma and Myth: A Theological Debate*. Edited by Hans Werner Bartsch. Translated by Reginald H. Fuller. London: S.P.C.K. (1953), pp. 138-174.

Tillich, Paul. *Systematic Theology*. Volume I. Chicago: The University of Chicago Press, 1951.

Tillich, Paul. *Dynamics of Faith*. New York: Harper & Row, 1957.

Todorov, Tzvetan. "On Linguistic Symbolism," in *New Literary History*, Vol. 6, No. 1 (1974), pp. 111-134.

Todorov, Tzvetan. *Symbolism and Interpretation*. Ithaca: Cornell University Press, 1982.

The Holy Bible. Revised Standard Version. New York: Thomas Nelson & Sons, 1952.

von Wright, Georg H. *An Essay in Modal Logic.* Amsterdam: North-Holland Publishing Company, 1951.

von Wright, Georg H. "A New System of Deontic Logic," in *Deontic Logic: Introductory and Systematic Readings.* Edited by Risto Hilpnien. Dordrecht: D. Reidel Publishing Company, 1971.

Ware, Jr., James H. *Not with Words of Wisdom: Performative Language and Liturgy.* Washington, D.C.: University Press of America, 1981.

Wellman, Carl. *The Language of Ethics.* Cambridge: Harvard University Press, 1961.

Whitehead, Alfred North. *Process and Reality: An Essay in Cosmology.* New York: The Free Press, 1978.

Wimsatt, Jr., W.K. *The Verbal Icon: Studies in the Meaning of Poetry.* University of Kentucky: University of Kentucky Press, 1954.

Wittgenstein, Ludwig. *Tractatus Logico-Philosophicus.* Translated by C.K. Ogden. Mineola: Dover Publications, 1999.

Zwingli, Ulrich. "On Baptism," "On the Lord's Supper," and "An Exposition of the Faith," in *Zwingli and Bullinger.* Edited and translated by G.W. Bromley. Philadelphia: The Westminster Press, 1953.

978-0-595-42409-2
0-595-42409-0

Printed in the United Kingdom by
Lightning Source UK Ltd., Milton Keynes
136843UK00002B/254/A